Representation Matters

Becoming an anti-racist educator

Aisha Thomas

BLOOMSBURY EDUCATION

LONDON   OXFORD   NEW YORK   NEW DELHI   SYDNEY

BLOOMSBURY EDUCATION
Bloomsbury Publishing Plc
50 Bedford Square, London, WC1B 3DP, UK
29 Earlsfort Terrace, Dublin 2, Ireland

BLOOMSBURY, BLOOMSBURY EDUCATION and the Diana logo are trademarks of
Bloomsbury Publishing Plc

First published in Great Britain, 2022 by Bloomsbury Publishing Plc

A catalogue record for this book is available from the British Library

ISBN: PB: 978-1-4729-8945-1; ePDF: 978-1-4729-8946-8; ePub: 978-1-4729-8947-5

2 4 6 8 10 9 7 5 3 (paperback)

Typeset by Newgen KnowledgeWorks Pvt. Ltd., Chennai, India
Printed and bound in the UK by CPI Group (UK) Ltd., Croydon, CR0 4YY

To find out more about our authors and books visit www.bloomsbury.com
and sign up for our newsletters

'Love is an action, never simply a feeling.' bell hooks

In honour of the late bell hooks I want to acknowledge the sentiment that is quoted here. Love is an action. The work to include and create a sense of belonging isn't just about making changes; it is doing something beyond intention, something that impacts the lives of the othered. The work should be rooted in kindness and love and centred around understanding ourselves and how our actions impact the world around us.

Contents

Acknowledgements

To all the contributors who have shared their knowledge, experience, wisdom, guidance and vulnerability, I thank you with all my heart. I could not have written this book without you. You are a phenomenal set of educators and the children you have taught and guided are so blessed to have had you in their lives.

To all the educators who have supported me along this journey, I wouldn't be the woman I am today if it wasn't for all of the help and support that you have given me.

To my ancestors who endured so much so that I could be, thank you. I hope I have made you proud.

To my friends and family, thank you for putting up with me as I have written this book. Being dyslexic meant that this book was no easy feat, yet you were patient and kind.

To my faith, I give thanks and praise to the almighty. There have been moments when I didn't think I could do it and you have given me the strength to pull through.

To Raekwon, Larenz, Talia and Taite, Aunty is doing all she can to make a better pathway for you.

To my boys, Tacari and Avishae, thank you for being my reason and my inspiration. Everything I do is for you. Mummy loves you.

*

This book has been written for every educator who has the responsibility, privilege and opportunity to change a life.

This book is for every child who has grown up in a society where they have had to question their worthiness because of the colour of their skin.

#RepresentationMatters

*

To everyone reading, thank you for taking this journey with me. It is not always easy to hold up the mirror and make change. But it is the only way that we will dismantle the current systems of oppression.

With love and light,
Aisha x

Introduction

I started writing this book in 2019 as a 35-year-old assistant principal; the world was different back then (it feels like it was a decade ago!). It was before the Covid-19 pandemic and before the resurgence of race relations in the UK. This book has taken me on a journey, and I am not the woman who started writing just a few short years ago. I have always been passionate about inclusion and diversity work; it is the natural activist in me. I wanted to be heard, seen and included. I identify as Black British; my heritage is Jamaican. Following my mum's ancestry, I think we originate from West Africa, primarily Nigeria. It is all I know at the moment, as I couldn't trace further back than my great-great-grandparents. Enslavement erased the rest of it.

Representation Matters: Becoming an anti-racist educator was never a book I planned to write. However, the more I embarked upon my mission to challenge the education system with regards to its racial inequalities, the more I became aware of the lack of resources available to educators who wanted to challenge themselves both personally and professionally. I read leadership book after leadership book… no mention of race. I read books on teaching standards… again, no mention of race. I read books about pedagogy, behaviour, teaching and learning, yet struggled to find many books that spoke about race. So, how does a teacher, trainee, teaching assistant, pastoral support worker or school leader embark on this journey?

I see this book as an opportunity to amplify the voices of the marginalised and ensure that their authentic lived experiences are told. They are the most affected by the systemic racism that exists in our education system today. Yet they continue to be silenced and gaslighted. Listening to their experiences is as good a starting point as any for all educators wanting to rethink representation.

My journey to rethinking representation

There are a million ways in which I could have started this book. In the end I decided to start at the very beginning: why representation matters to me and how it has affected my journey in education. However, to understand my world view, I need to go back to the source, the root of my experience. My understanding of representation starts with my foundations: my upbringing, and the funds of knowledge and the parental capital that I was blessed with. It has also been shaped by the experiences I have had as a professional.

This book is named after my company, Representation Matters Ltd©, which was launched in July 2020. While the company may be relatively new, the work isn't. It started a decade earlier, when a young man in prison challenged me to rethink representation.

Before transitioning into education, I had a brief career in law. I read law at university and then worked as a legal assistant for a few years before being offered a training contract to become a solicitor. Whilst working as a legal assistant in a Bristol law firm, I became a volunteer peer mentor for the Prince's Trust. The project I supported was called the National Offender Management Scheme (NOMS) and its purpose was to help young men back into the community following a period in prison. This was an emotional experience. I had always been aware of the disproportionate numbers of Black and Brown children and young people in prison. However, this was the first time that I had seen the physical manifestation of these statistics. I felt an overwhelming sense of responsibility and I wanted to do all I could to make a difference.

There was a particular moment in time that is still very vivid in my memory. I was being escorted from one side of the prison yard to the meeting room for my session. I found myself in the middle of a 'mass move'. A 'mass move' is when all prisoners are moved to various locations across the site. Before I knew it, I was surrounded by a sea of faces. I was scared; I was overwhelmed. But what struck me the most was that I was surrounded by Black and Brown young men. I couldn't help questioning how this could be. Why were there so many? What was happening to our Black and Brown children and young people?

After the 'mass move', I went to meet one of my mentees. During our conversation about the future and next steps, he said to me that perhaps if I had been his teacher, he wouldn't be in prison today. He didn't mean literally me, but what it represented to see a Black person in power, a decision-maker. What a difference that could have made to this young person, and many others like him, who just longed to see himself in a different role.

He then talked about representation and explained that all the people in power are White. He talked about only seeing himself in sport, media and crime. I look back on this moment and I realise it was a catalyst for change. I didn't want to be part of the system that would see him go to prison. Instead, I wanted to be part of a system that could prevent young people like him from following this pathway in the first place. I had to get the young people at an earlier point. So, what better career than education? This is where my journey began.

What you will find in this book

Ultimately, I want this book to be a beacon of truth; one which heralds a new reality. My hope is that it will help those who want to start their own journey, those who misunderstand why representation in education is important and those who want to bring about true, lasting change. The book has been written with all educators in mind, from early career teachers to experienced teachers and school leaders. It is essential to note that most of the content in this book was formulated pre-2020, before the pandemic and before the death of George Floyd. I was a serving assistant principal, leading on high-level behaviour needs, safeguarding and school culture. This book is not a reaction to recent events for me or for the educators who have contributed their words. It is a response to a lifelong experience. I write through the lens of my authentic lived experience as a Black woman. I am dyslexic and was diagnosed at the age of 21, which also forms part of my intersectional lens.

Just like me, your world view, your understanding of the world and your understanding of representation will have been shaped by your personal experiences from early childhood through to adolescence and adulthood, as well as your professional experiences as an educator. This is why I advocate that real change comes from within. It starts with deep self-reflection and honesty. You need to understand your starting point as an individual – what representation means to you and why – before you can begin to implement change as an educator. I often talk about the concept of triple consciousness. The original theory of triple consciousness has been discussed by Sara Lomax-Reese and Nahum Welang, who examined the intersection of race, nationality and gender. They were inspired by W. E. B. Du Bois' theory of double consciousness, which argued that Black women see themselves through the lens of both gender and race (Pelt-Willis, 2021). As educators, we have three aspects to our selves that each interact with one another throughout our lives and professional careers:

1. The person you are at home.

2. The person you are at work.

3. The person you are expected to be in education.

As educators, it is important that we take time to think about who we are at home. This will impact on what we do, what we say and how we show up in the classroom. It will also impact on our journey towards inclusive and anti-racist practices in school and how much of this we choose to implement. But most importantly, it will impact on how we engage with children and young people. How often have you let your beliefs impact your behaviour in the classroom, the corridor or the playground?

and to be anti-racist. But the reality is that it takes time, effort and commitment. Grand initiatives, black squares, flags and heritage month celebrations will only do so much. Instead of offering a checklist, I therefore want this book to guide you through a process towards transformation. This is not a step-by-step handbook of actions to undertake, but a series of self-reflection questions, activities, discussion points for staff meetings, support, coaching and guidance to help you begin your journey and set you on a path of deeper reflection and positive change as an individual, an educator and a school community. Work through the activities and questions, taking time to reflect and make notes, and explore the discussion points with colleagues in meetings and training sessions. In each chapter, I will also share some of the experiences of my fellow comrades, all of whom have volunteered their time and energy, and re-lived their trauma, to ensure that we can do better for the children we serve.

This book should put you in a space of deep reflection, enabling you to hold up a mirror to yourself to think about who you are as an individual and who you are as an educator. This is not supposed to be an easy journey. It requires bravery and dedication, and if you are working through this process as a department or whole school, a culture of psychological safety is paramount.

A note about language

The ability to racialise me and describe myself has always been a point of contention. I apologise to any Black person or Person of Colour who is triggered by the experiences or the terms I am about to share. When I was younger, I experienced anti-Blackness and was referred to as a 'coconut' on more than one occasion. Black on the outside and White on the inside. When I attended my majority-White secondary school, I was too Black for the people there. Yet when I returned to my local area, which was very diverse, some people in my community felt I was too *White* for them. This, coupled with my skin tone, was very confusing for me. I felt I had to code-switch as I got on and off the school bus.

My skin complexion has played a part in this and I have been referred to as 'browning', 'lighty' and 'redskin'. These are just some of the terms I can reference here. There were also many others that I will not name, but I will say that when I also had straight, relaxed hair, it was common for me to be asked if I was mixed or if I had any Indian heritage. When working at one particular educational establishment, a member of staff challenged me for calling myself Black and said that she would call me 'latte'. I wasn't proper Black. So, I question what this means for me.

I am of Jamaican heritage; however, I have never lived in Jamaica and neither have my parents. Yet my Jamaican heritage has had such an impact on my life. I identify as Black British, but that is also only part of my identity. Whilst Africa is my roots, that has been erased and I have been stripped of that part of my identity. I have no idea where my family would have originated from before they were enslaved.

I have been challenged many times about language and some have said don't use Black while others say do use Black. Some have said to refer to myself as Jamaican, Caribbean and African. Some have said race is a social construct and isn't real, so I should identify by my ethnicity. We now have many terms: People of Colour, BIPOC (Black, Indigenous and People of Colour), Black and Brown people, Political Blackness, Global Majority and Melanin Rich. All have nuances and complexities, and each person who is a part of these communities will have their own preferences about which terms to use to describe themselves and the people around them. Personally, I identify as a Black woman and choose to racially identify in that way.

In this book, I will use the terms Black, Brown, racially minoritised and People of Colour. I appreciate that not everyone will choose to identify in these ways and I respect the individual choices of the reader. The terms Black, Brown and White have been capitalised throughout the book to refer to race, ethnicity and culture. For more on this, read Chapter 5 of Blair Imani's book *Read This to Get Smarter* (2021). Please note that the writers who have contributed lived experience pieces are using the terms they feel most comfortable with, so other language will appear in some of the chapters. In addition, research papers and data sources often use BAME (Black, Asian and minority ethnic) or BME (Black and minority ethnic). These terms will therefore be reproduced in certain places in the book in order to capture the data as accurately as possible.

The transformation process

So, what does the transformation process I hope to guide you through look like? I have broken it up into three distinct parts, which form a framework for the chapters in this book:

1. Reflecting and reviewing

2. Listening and decentring

3. Creating an action plan

Let's look at each of these in more detail.

Reflecting and reviewing

As mentioned, the first step when beginning this work is to start with *you*. Think about who you are, your core beliefs and values, where you grew up, where your knowledge base has come from and what your influences have been throughout your life. **Chapter 1** explores this process of self-reflection in more detail.

Another step at this initial stage is to review and audit all aspects of your practice and your department or school as a whole (if you are doing this work at a departmental or whole-school level). This will include curriculum, staffing, data, physical environment, policies, processes, website and the work of the children and young people. You want to take a deep dive into your school and hold the lens of race in front of you. Use data which is both qualitative and quantitative. Facts and numbers will provide a base line and foundational starting point which you can use to measure progress. The voices of your pupils and your school community will provide authentic lived experience. **Chapter 2** will support you in this process.

Listening and decentring

Seeking feedback from pupils and the wider school community is not only a crucial part of the data gathering you undertake but also a vital element in your own reflective journey. A real sense of community will come from listening to the voices of those you serve. You will learn so much from the children and young people in your school. We often assume that we, as educators, are teaching them. However, their lived experiences can teach us. We must also be aware of the generational gap. Our lived experiences can often be very different to those of the pupils we serve today. The accessibility of the internet and social media has transformed the way in which children and young people are learning. Even when we are not ready to have the conversation, they are. We need to be prepared to listen and understand.

Listening to your whole school community, children and young people, governors, staff, parents and carers, and partner schools will not only create a sense of connection, but it will also provide a deeper understanding of the temperature of your school community. Pay close attention to what is highlighted and what is not referenced. It may be telling you a story that you have not noticed before. **Chapters 3 and 4** will consider in more detail how we talk to students about race and at what age we should start talking to children about race and racism.

Listening to the voices of the children in your school will shape your perspectives and support you in thinking about race and representation through a new lens. As part of this process, we will consider how we can move away from centring Whiteness, thinking again about the language we use when we talk about race (**Chapter 5**) and the importance of children having a diverse range of adult role models in their lives (**Chapter 6**).

The titles of Chapters 1 to 6 each pose a 'big question' to support the process of self-reflection in these initial two stages of the transformation process. Before you start to read each chapter, take a moment to reflect on how you would answer the big question being posed. Jot down your initial response to the question. After you have read the chapter, revisit your response and think about whether you would now answer the question in a different way or if there is anything you would add or take away.

Creating an action plan

It is important that you have a clear strategy and plan of action for the work you wish to undertake. Be clear and intentional about your priorities and how you will carry out your work. You want to ensure that the vision is shared and that the why is clear. We often want to jump to the how, as that is where the work takes place. But what you will do and why you will do it are just as important. The action plan shouldn't be an add-on; it should be woven into the school's culture. Using your values and misson to develop an ethos that's inclusive will help to embed the practice.

An action plan will include what steps you will take, your success criteria, milestones, staff responsibilities and resources required. Reflect on the following questions and use them to structure a written strategy document:

- Who is leading on the work strategically and operationally?
- Where are your champions?
- Who will be your critical friend?
- Whose voices are being heard?

- What are your priorities?
- At what level is the work being done?
- How will you hold yourself to account?
- How will you evidence your journey?
- Where will you obtain support?
- What budget and resource will you provide?
- If a Black person or Person of Colour is leading on the work, how are you protecting them?
- Is the work embedded throughout the school or is the focus only on the curriculum?
- What structures will you put in place to allow for challenge?
- Where is the operational work happening?
- Is the work embedded in your overall plans for your school?

The third section of this book will cover some important areas for you to examine and consider as part of your action plan, from the legal framework (**Chapter 7**) to implementing inclusive practice (**Chapter 9**), challenging overt and covert racism (**Chapter 10**), decolonising the curriculum (**Chapter 11**), PSHE (**Chapter 12**) and working with parents and caregivers (**Chapter 13**).

A core part of the action plan is teacher training (**Chapter 8**). Ensure that all staff (including you) have adequate resources and training to deliver and achieve your action plan and fulfil your strategy. It is important for all staff to have a baseline understanding of, for example, the Equality Act 2010, bias in education and key terminology and shared language regarding inclusion, anti-discrimination and anti-racist practice. Too often staff are given one-off or annual training that is never put into practice. Allow space for different styles of learning. Training could be offered through:

- external sessions
- internal sessions
- reading
- podcasts
- articles
- videos
- conferences

- conversation circles
- TeachMeets
- curriculum challenge and planning sessions.

Remember to analyse how effective this training is. How are teachers putting CPD into practice? What steps are they taking? How are you measuring impact? What changes are you seeing in your students?

As you are implementing your action plan, take the necessary steps to review the impact of what you are doing. Ensure that the team of staff and children who are supporting the journey are a part of this process. Take a moment to pause, reflect and track the work that has taken place. Talk to marginalised groups to temperature check change and consider any areas where further work is needed. Review your progress, critique the evidence and don't be afraid to pivot if necessary. Your action plan is a breathing document and should be treated as such. Ensure you have identified key staff to evaluate progress and hold the work to account. It's important that this isn't the same person who is responsible operationally. Clearly defined roles are key.

As you work through the transformation process, think about how you will ensure that the work you are doing lasts. This is our legacy: the seeds that we sow today to reap tomorrow. Work of this nature takes time and there is no finish line. Instead you need stamina to keep going. Putting in place a strong framework will ensure the work is embedded and ever evolving, but how do you create sustainable change that will continue for generations to come? What methodology will you choose? Is it championing curriculum change, conducting annual reviews, or holding regular student voice sessions? Targets, equality impact assessment and tailored lesson observations can help. Some settings may also want to achieve charter marks and awards to recognise and acknowledge their success. Whatever you decide, ensure that the work is the golden thread in your practice and in your school. Create that energy, so whoever walks into your building feels a sense of connection, belonging and pride. It is time to take a stand and stop being complicit in tokenistic gestures, pointless policy-writing and annual tick-box training. It is time for true, lasting change. We owe it to ourselves and we owe it to future generations. So let us begin.

PART 1

Reflecting and reviewing

1 Why does representation matter?

'When you are accustomed to privilege, equality feels like oppression.'

Oscar Auliq-Ice (2019)

For me, the response to this question is that it depends. The answer you get is only as good as the context of the question. Representation can sometimes be used as a tool to mask and shy away from the real *work* that needs to be done. Therefore, it is important to understand the way in which the term 'representation' is being used. I could suggest that a room of children is representative, without giving due care and attention to whose voices are being heard, the impact of any silences and what this means for those in the space. It is important that all children can see themselves. We need to challenge the representation we see and integrate the circumstances surrounding it. Overrepresentation can be as damaging as underrepresentation.

But before we embark on this work, we must first consider what it is that we are trying to achieve and why. So, why does representation matter to you? The only way you can begin to answer this question is to look within and to think about yourself as an educator.

My own relationship with education is a strange one. Being a teacher herself, my mum was fiercely passionate about education. I remember spending days sitting in her classroom in awe of the knowledge that she was imparting to the children in front of her. I also wondered why she was so rare. She mainly taught in inner-city schools. Here were classrooms full of Black and Brown faces, yet for these children, seeing a teacher whose face matched theirs was a novelty. Of course, when a behavioural concern arose, out came an army of Black- and Brown-faced support in the roles of teaching assistant, dinner person, caretaker, cleaner. I wonder what this did to my young mind. Did I ever envisage that a person who looked like me could be in a position of authority? Or were people like me merely there to support and reinforce the status quo?

Activity: How diverse is your workforce?

Take a moment to think about your current school or academy. What does the ethnic diversity look like in your workforce? Note down your thoughts in the table below. You could include numbers or statistics if these are available to you or simply your own reflections.

Leadership (CEO, senior leaders, middle leaders, heads of faculty)	Teachers	Associate staff (including catering staff, estate teams, cleaners)	Governors or board

My lived experience

I only had one Black teacher in my entire educational experience. I realise now how damaging that was for my development. I attended a multicultural primary school, before attending a secondary school which was predominately White and middle class. For the first time in my life, I realised I was Black – and I realised it was an issue. There were many comments that made it clear I was different. One particular moment that still haunts me today is when a friend of mine said to me, 'You cannot come to my house because you are Black.' I think back now to the microaggressions and overt racism I experienced, completely unaware of what it was doing to my psyche.

'Here comes trouble' on seeing me simply walking down the corridor.
'Where do you come from?' 'Easton.' 'No… really, where do you come from?'
'Why is your hair so coarse?'
'Why do you moisturise your skin?'
'Rough where you live… people get stabbed.'

'You can't come to my house… my mum said we can be friends at school, but you can't come to my house.'

Little did I know, this experience was training me to navigate my way through institutional racism. The same system that still exists today. What hurts more than the racism I experienced at school is that my children are having these same experiences in their own education.

As I mentioned, I had one Black teacher while I was at school, but I did not have a great relationship with her. Looking back now, it was clear she didn't want the weight of my Blackness on her shoulders. A burden that I understand as an educator today.

As an educator, my personal experiences of racism and bias have been varied:

- A colleague called me her 'coffee-coloured friend' then decided that perhaps I was a 'latte'. I challenged her and stated that I identify as Black, only to be told, 'I don't care what you say. You are not Black.' She then referred to a student and said, 'Now he's Black, so Black he's scary.'

- A super head told me that I was one of the 'good EAL' and congratulated me on understanding English and settling so well into British culture. I speak no other language and was born here.

These lived experiences demonstrate the impact of overt racism, but what we mustn't do is neglect to discuss the subtle, the unconscious, the 'I do not see colour' type of racism. The microaggressions that lead to othering. When I complete an equality form, for example, I can only select Black African or Black Caribbean. I do not have the option of choosing Black British. Yet my parents were born here, and I was born here. How many generations of my family need to live here before I can select Black – Black British?

I often ask myself why it took me so long to wake up, to see it. To answer that I need to take a step back to assess my funds of knowledge.

It's hard not to be emotional when I write this, as my commitment to education is not just professional, it's personal too. Integral to my world view is my experience of motherhood. My various roles as granddaughter, daughter and mother have all affected the way I view the world and my relationship with representation. It carries with it the physical weight of my ancestors. A weight laden with toxicity. A weight which has been inherited and passed on, generation after generation.

For me, the word representation is so intrinsically linked with the words strong, female and Black that I cannot look at the word in isolation. It is the intersectionality of all three that compounds my experience.

So, what do I mean? Let us cast our minds back to 'Mammy Two Shoes', the fictional character from MGM's cartoon *Tom and Jerry*. She presents as a heavy-set, middle-aged

African American who has the responsibility of caring for the home. Interestingly, but unsurprisingly, this is the image I see when I think of both of my grandmothers leading their households and raising their children. In the character of Mammy Two Shoes, we see the 'representation' of motherhood in the mainstream. This was my first example of leadership and command. The idea that the woman must demonstrate and exude strength and stability, ensuring, above all else, that she keeps everything together. In other words: the Black matriarch. She needs to cook, clean, tidy and work all the hours God sends to make ends meet. She needs to sit and scrub clothes until her hands are sore. She needs to miss meals to ensure that we all eat.

She exists only to serve.

She exists to sacrifice herself.

Servitude is a quality that I have carried with me into my role as an assistant principal: I am there to make sacrifices and serve the community I work within. I seek validation from those around me to ensure that my work is good enough to meet the standards – standards set by them. This might sound innocuous but in fact it is dangerous. I can lose sight of my value as an individual. 'Aisha' seems to exist somewhere between assistant principal and Miss Thomas; lost, perhaps.

So, what role does my Blackness play in this? I was frequently told that I had to work five times harder to succeed, as my Blackness would come with a weight that my White counterparts would never have to carry. So, I developed a double consciousness: the version of me at work and the version of me at home. I would be the first to arrive and the last to leave, just to prove my worth, to justify my position. Getting the job done could never be enough – I had to demonstrate my hard work.

However, the most confusing element to me was the absence of the man. What was his role? On one hand, all the women in my family were fierce feminists: 'Be strong', 'Don't rely on any man', 'Make your own money', 'You can do whatever a man can do', 'You don't need a man', 'As a Black woman, you'll always need to work harder.' But on the other hand, we were being raised to serve men, to be at their beck and call. The boys would sit there while women washed their clothes, cooked their food and catered to their every whim.

How much has this learnt behaviour transferred into my professional practice? How much has it become a subconscious need to serve the male seniors above me? I must meet their needs and demands. But where does this stem from?

Only a few generations ago, my family members would have been slaves. Whilst men and women had an equally devastating experience of slavery (they both suffered the most severe torture and pain; they were both torn away from their homelands; they both suffered physical, spiritual and mental torture), the roles and experiences of women were different. While men were owned for their strength, colonies turned purchased females into field-hands; not only were they readily available, but crucially they were cheaper. Eventually female slaves outnumbered the men. Forcing them to work meant they lost their predetermined role. In Africa, a woman's primary role was that of mother. In slavery, this role was debased. In Africa, childbirth was a rite of passage. For enslaved women within the American plantation system, it signified something else. It earned them increased respect – or value. Being able to produce their own slaves gave a slave owner an economic advantage.

The psychological damage suffered by these women was irreparable. Women were expected to put the needs of the master and his family before their own children. The slave mother returning to the plantation after childbirth had to leave her children to be raised by others. Her role as mother became another task, in addition to her position as a slave.

The psychological need to serve has, I believe, been transferred at a cellular level. As Resmaa Menakem (2021) says in his book *My Grandmother's Hands*, 'Our bodies exist in the present. To your thinking brain, there is past, present, and future, but to a traumatised body there is only *now*. That *now* is the home of intense survival energy.' I recognise many of these traits in my leadership style and behaviour today. As a single mother, in particular, my children pay the price for this leadership style. They attend school, they go to breakfast club and after-school club, whilst I meet the needs of others, letting others raise my children. These were necessary sacrifices that I felt compelled to make: missing important events, cancelling birthday parties, skipping homework, just to ensure that I showed up. It's what I needed to do, right? Work five times as hard, always show up – even at a cost to my own family.

Some history accounts state that while their male counterparts tried to escape, slave mothers often stayed in bondage. This also seems to be replicated in society today. Why is it that we have made so much sacrifice, yet we continue to be underrepresented?

I would not be the mother I am today, the activist, the assistant principal or educational consultant, if it were not for standing on the shoulders of my ancestors. Whilst this leadership journey has not been easy – and there is much more work and reflection to do – I am proud of the amazing Black woman that I am today. However, I cannot help but ask the question: would my experiences have been different if there was more representation?

Lived experience: Samara Cameron, SEN class teacher

Allow me to set the scene. A little girl from Zaire has to move with her family to France. She asks her dad about the football final she will miss, and her dad fills her with the hope that she could play for France if she is any good. Her immediate reaction is: 'Seen many Blacks on the French team?' Fast forward a few scenes, and the same girl is in front of the television watching France in their starting line-up, and a Black player appears on her screen. Her face lights up... End scene. Well, not quite.

In my opinion, the 2016 film this scene is taken from, *The African Doctor*, is a story that embodies why representation matters. It forced me to question my understanding of representation and why it's so fundamental within an educational context.

In 2018, a policy paper was published to explain the duty to 'increase diversity in the teaching workforce' (Department for Education and Race Disparity Unit, 2018). The paper intended to show that although there is now more diversity than ever, there is still room for vast improvement when it involves teachers from minority backgrounds. Looking solely at Black teachers (including 'Black/other') within education, they make up 2.5 per cent of the overall workforce in comparison to White British teachers who make up 84.7 per cent (Department for Education, 2021a). Furthermore, there appears to be a large disparity between gender: there are significantly more Black female teachers than male.

As we live in a continually evolving society, there should be a fair and balanced representation of ethnic groups generally, but especially in education.

A part of representation, in my opinion, is identity and modelling. So much of how a person is fabricated is based on their identity and perspective of self. Siraj-Blatchford and Clarke (2000) believe that how children view themselves is learned and imitated by what they see exhibited to them. This begins to form in children's developmental ages, so by the ages of three and four, children are able to identify the differences between themselves and those around them.

My deep sense of identity stems from my first teachers, my parents, who cultivated a deep regard and respect for learning. My father, who was born and schooled in Jamaica, brought a pride and acknowledgement of how education plays an integral part in success in life. My mother (from Jamaican heritage) grew up and was schooled in England, which came with completely different challenges and perspectives than my father had experienced. My parents were instrumental in giving me the confidence and support to achieve and to overcome all the challenges they knew I might face in a system not designed for me. Together they instilled a common understanding that education is fundamental to having choices – and choices give you power.

At the other end of the spectrum, far from my personal experience of representation, is my educational experience and the lack of representation within this. Having a strong sense of self is only part of why representation is important. The first time I encountered a Black teacher was when I was 17. He was a Black man. Without him, I am unsure that I would have completed my year of study, and therefore the rest of my journey would have been very different. Better representation of Black teachers within an educational context provokes a sense of belonging, understanding and community.

Taking a minute aspect such as pupil exclusions, the highest exclusion rates are from Gypsy, Roma and Traveller pupils, followed by mixed White and Black Caribbean, and Black Caribbean pupils – at nearly three times the amount compared to White British pupils (Department for Education, 2020a). I find that statistic to be alarming and distressing. It forces me to question why this is the case. Is there something to be said for the fact that only one per cent of teachers within the workforce are Black Caribbean? This is just one example of why there needs to be open, honest dialogue about race within classroom settings.

As an educator, I think it would be ignorant, even absurd, not to educate young people about race. Those discussions should be happening from the Early Years throughout the education system. Representation should not just apply to what children see physically, but it should stem from the books children read and the messages that are transmitted through the curriculum.

It pains me that in my experience schools don't use books that focus on children of colour or different cultures to teach the English curriculum. It particularly jars with me that many books for children under the age of five have animals or inanimate objects as their protagonists. If we are using the theory and notion that children are shaped and developed characteristically from an early age, then why isn't that translated in the texts used within their learning? It is infuriating that children have to wait until they are learning about a specific religion or a focused topic on, for example, the Amazon Rainforest to encounter ethnicity. Perhaps if we were using a more eclectic and diverse range of texts, young people would have more choice and option about who they want to become and how they want to be identified.

Some of the issues I have encountered when trying to change the familiarity of the texts being used in the curriculum are discomfort in racial literacy, laziness in approach and lack of resources. However, I believe it can be achieved.

The power of the scene from *The African Doctor* forces a narrative that is obligatory in the way education is seen and developed. By seeing representation, the girl has a physical depiction of hope and aspiration. It gives her a choice. In my opinion, that is what I am supposed to do as an educator: allowing children to make informed decisions.

Samara Cameron is a passionate experienced teacher who has taught in various boroughs and has covered all year groups of the primary sector. Currently, Samara is a primary SEN teacher.

What are *your* perceptions of race and representation?

Imagine a world where racial superiority is stripped of its crown and children are treated with equal importance. The reality is that this isn't the experience for Black, Brown and racially minoritised children in education. Often educators will state that they do not see colour and they treat all children equally. The truth is that we *do* see colour; we see and experience culture and we acknowledge that we are different. However, the issue occurs when a child is treated differently, when a child is marginalised, when a child is unable to attain and when a child is unsafe because of their skin.

Conversations about race and representation are not new. They have been present for years and have shapeshifted and manifested in educational discourse in many ways. Yet these conversations, particularly when discussed in the context of racism, are often treated with resistance and a sense of awkwardness. There is deflection and a tendency to open the space for 'whataboutery', for example: 'What about White working-class children?' The truth is that education has often been the place where many examples of racial oppression have taken place. We saw this in the seventies, when scores of Black children were treated as educationally 'subnormal', and we see this in our present-day education system where Black children are disproportionately represented in sanctions and exclusions.

It's easy to think of these issues as systemic and out of the hands of individual teachers, but every educator's biases, attitudes, thoughts and actions regarding race will impact on the manifestation of racism in our schools. We all have a responsibility to unpack our own understanding of race and racism and consider our own perceptions of racial identities. This is the first step in moving towards anti-racist practice.

This can be a difficult conversation, as we often do not wish to lean into our own feelings, emotions and physical reactions when discussing race and the impact of racism. We are aware of the internal monologue that is happening in our minds when we are listening or talking and we feel our bodies reacting physically. This is part of the process, so notice these feelings and be prepared to move forward in spite of them.

bell hooks talked about the need for teachers to be actively involved and committed to a process of self-actualisation and self-reflection, which will support the development of their wellbeing and empower the students that they teach.

It is therefore important that, as educators, we take time to think about who we are. It will impact on what we do, say and how we show up in the classroom. It will also impact on how we engage with learning about anti-racism, and how much of this we choose to implement. But most importantly, it will impact on how we engage with children and young people. How often have you let your beliefs impact your behaviour in school?

I challenge you to hold up the mirror and consider who you are. Grab a piece of paper and map out your answers.

Who are you?

I would like you to consider:

- your core beliefs and values
- where you grew up
- where your knowledge base has come from
- your influences
- your education
- your parents or carers
- your accepted labels in regard to race, religion, gender and sexuality.

I now want to refer back to the theory I call the triple consciousness (see page 3). Take a look at the answers you wrote down for the question above. Would you change any of these answers if you were looking through each of the following lenses?

1. The person you are at home.
2. The person you are at work.
3. The person you are expected to be in education.

What are the differences between your three personas and why do you think this is? For me, when considering this question and the work of bell hooks, I think deeply about the parts of me I felt I had to leave at the school gate.

Let's now move into thinking specifically about your racial identity.

How are you racialised?

I would like you to consider:

- How do others racialise you?
- How do you wish to racialise yourself?
- Would you consider yourself to be British? Or perhaps English, Welsh, Scottish or Irish?
- If none of the above, how would you describe yourself?

Now try this one:

When did you first realise you were racialised?

I would like you to consider:

- When did it happen?
- Where did it happen?
- Was it a positive or negative experience?
- Did this realisation change your behaviour?

For Black, Brown and racially minoritised people, this will often happen early on in their childhood and in unpleasant circumstances. Yet for White people, this will often happen later in life and in a very different context. The reality is race is a social construct. It is not real and it has no biological basis. Yet we live in a world where race has been used to create hierarchy and dominance in modern society. The construct of race is responsible for the enslavement of millions of Africans, and we are living the consequence of this today. Yet racism is still treated by many as something that can be contested. We see it every day; we just accept the status quo and ignore it. It is acceptable racism that we simply tolerate.

So how do we move forward from here?

We need to start by being *honest*. Race must be a social construct, but we see it, feel it and hear it. It shows up in all aspects of life. Acknowledgement of racism is the beginning and grappling with the idea of being non-racist may be your first step. But what action are you taking to be anti-racist? How does this become automatic and embedded? How do you ensure you are racially literate?

It takes a commitment to learning and unlearning. You need to think about the knowledge you access and the diet of information you continue to access. You need racial stamina, a commitment to keep going. Even when you are at your weakest and most exhausted, you need to remember that there is someone, perhaps even yourself, with a lived experience that they can't turn off.

This final activity is inspired by Photo Voice, which is a visual methodology and qualitative research tool developed in 1992 by Caroline Wang at the University of Michigan and Mary Ann Burris with the Ford Foundation China. It was developed as a tool for social activism, based on an idea that stories created with photography and words can powerfully express and represent different communities.

What does anti-racist practice mean to you in education?

I would like you to consider this question and take a photo or find an image which expresses your answer.

Use the imagery to explain how racism manifests for you. Define how you see race and racism, how it shows up in your life, in your teaching and in your educational career, and what can be done to bring about positive change.

Try this as a team activity and compare your image with that of your colleagues. This will provide deep insight into where you are on your journey, but also an understanding of where your colleagues are on their journey, and where you can go next.

Some definitions: race, ethnicity, nationalism, heritage and culture

I want to end this chapter with the definitions of some important words that you will encounter on your journey towards anti-racist practice, so you can use them appropriately. I am grateful to Dr Matt Jacobs for his help with this section.

Race

Race is a social construct that categorises people based on reductive ideas of phenotypical or observable physical difference, for example, skin colour, hair texture or eye colour. The term 'race' was first used to differentiate between humans during the eighteenth century when English imperialists developed a hierarchy of peoples, separating themselves as superior to the indigenous peoples of the lands they colonised. 'Race' gained a scientific legitimisation in the nineteenth century as 'Enlightenment era' scientists imbued the term with a false biological or genetic aspect that was used to create a hierarchy of peoples, at the top of which they placed White Europeans. This 'science' was used to justify exploitation, oppression and murder in the form of expanded imperialism and slavery.

As more modern science has debunked the myths of the Enlightenment era, showing that there is no biological basis for the differentiation of peoples along the lines of race, its meaning and use have evolved to take on an aspect of cultural differentiation. We now see hierarchies of cultural value associated with phenotypical differences, whether these be specific cultural practices of indigenous peoples, or the association of negative behavioural traits to people categorised as being from a specific 'race'.

Ethnicity

Ethnicity is often mistakenly associated exclusively with People of Colour, particularly in its use in 'official' terms such as Black, Asian, and Minority Ethnic but equally when White people refer to 'ethnic clothes' or 'ethnic food'. However, ethnicity is a term that refers to any group of people who share an intersection of several factors of identity. These factors can include phenotypical differences but also a shared geography, history and culture. As such, there are a range of ethnicities within the White population. For example, we can talk about a Cornish ethnicity. Whilst the origins of 'ethnicity' as a term are rooted in the early colonial census taken by the British to further categorise and 'rank' indigenous people, more recent discussion has incorporated an element of self-identification into the idea of an ethnic identity, linking it to a sense of affinity with others who share a geography, history and culture.

Nationalism

Nationalism is born of a context in which a single ethnic or cultural group defines and retains both value and power within a geographic boundary. It is the myths, symbols and practices of this ethnic core that define not just the history of the nation but also the criteria for national identity. The geographic space across which a nation state is created is a historically contested territory and it is through the construction of the 'people' as a political community that that national sentiment is engendered.

Heritage

Heritage combines history and cultural practices of ethnicities. Heritage is often associated with physical objects, whether these be structures or artefacts of some kind linked to cultures and ethnicities, but it is also understood as including intangible cultural heritage, such as oral traditions, visual arts, literature and social practices.

Culture

In simple terms, culture refers to a 'system of meanings' that are articulated through a range of media, behaviours and activities that a group of people understand and perform on a day-to-day basis. Notions of culture and cultural value are intertwined with conceptions of race, ethnicity and nationality. The cultural characteristics of the dominant ethnicity within a nation are normalised and infused with social value and moral worth. The performance of the normalised cultural practices leads to the accruing of privileges whereas the negative moral evaluations of 'other' cultural practices lead to discrimination and exclusion.

Summary

Key learning points

- Unpacking our own understanding of race and racism and considering our own perceptions of racial identities is an essential starting point in our journey towards anti-racism.
- It's important to recognise how racial biases manifest in our attitudes, thoughts and actions.
- We must lean into our feelings, our emotions and our physical reactions when we are reflecting and speaking about race. Our bodies are talking to us.
- 'Microaggressions are everyday slights, insults, indignities and/or denigrating messages sent by well-intentioned people who are unaware of the hidden messages they communicate' (Derald Wing Sue). To understand more about the impact of microaggressions, I would recommend watching this short film: www.shots.net/news/view/new-film-cuts-to-the-heart-of-racist-micro-aggressions

Why does representation matter?

- 'Intersectionality' was a term coined in 1989 by Kimberlé Crenshaw, a civil rights activist and legal scholar. Crenshaw wrote that traditional feminist ideas and anti-racist policies exclude Black women because they face overlapping discrimination unique to them, arguing that the intersectional experience is greater than the sum of racism and sexism.

Key question

How often do you think about representation in your classroom?

a) Several times a day
b) Once a day
c) Several times a week
d) Once a month
e) Hardly ever

Why do you think this is?

Further self-reflection questions

1. How important are your early influences in characterising and developing your journey?
2. What aspect of your identity is least represented? Do you feel othered as a result?
3. Do you see racial representation – or the lack of – as an issue in your school?
4. What could you do to impact on the issue of representation in your school?

Discussion points for staff meetings

- Think about representation. How often do you see yourself represented in your working life?
- Share your experiences of representation and the impact that it has had on your life.
- How do we begin to implement the intent of increasing representation in education in order to make a real impact?

2 How important is the data?

'Data is a precious thing and will last longer than the systems themselves.'
Tim Berners-Lee (2006), inventor of the World Wide Web

The answer you get is only as good as the question you asked: when it comes to looking at data and ascertaining its importance, remember that it is subject to the lens and the context you are viewing it through.

In June 2020, Matt Hancock, who was Health Secretary at the time, defended the lack of Black MPs on the front bench and said the Cabinet was the most diverse in British history (Sky News). Reference was made to Chancellor Rishi Sunak and Home Secretary Priti Patel coming from 'ethnic' backgrounds. Using the term 'BAME' meant Hancock could argue that the Cabinet was indeed diverse. However, if the diversity is from one community, is it really diverse? At the time of the broadcast, there were 22 members of the cabinet. Six of them were female. None of them were Black or LGBT.

I have always struggled with data. It can be skewed to provide the narrative you are trying to portray, particularly when considering race and those racialised as Black. Schools and organisations can inflate figures and dilute the argument. The acronym 'BAME' (Black, Asian and minority ethnic) does just that. It's easy to demonstrate that you have a balance of diversity – if you include everyone who is not White British. But what does that do to individual communities? What does that do to those who are racially White in their native countries but are not British? The reality is that it creates erasure. It becomes problematic. Different groups of communities are put together in one big melting pot and treated like a monolith. Yet we know that there is so much richness and culture in individual communities, which should be explored and celebrated. However, we lose the opportunity for nuance and understanding when we misrepresent communities for the sake of data and box-ticking. How we manipulate the data can silence the most vulnerable voices.

In this chapter, we will examine what the data really says about the diversity of the teaching workforce. From two lived experiences, we will learn the true impact of a lack of diversity among school staff and we'll consider why the solution isn't as simple as hiring more teachers from minoritised backgrounds.

What does the data say about diversity in education?

In 2018, the Department for Education and the Race Disparity Unit published their 'statement of intent' document regarding the diversity of the teaching workforce. This document referenced that the teaching workforce is 'more diverse' than ever before. It stated that the current workforce reflected the increasing diversity of the country and its population. Yet this same report found that only eight per cent of teachers and three per cent of headteachers came from ethnic minority backgrounds. The data tells us that ethnic minority, LGBTQIA+ and disabled members of staff remain underrepresented and women remain underrepresented in school leadership positions.

So how is the teaching workforce more diverse? Or are we using the past as a benchmark? And if it is more varied than ever before, do we stop championing change?

Here's a snapshot of the national data in England in 2020.

- In total, there were approximately 461,090 classroom teachers, 48,130 deputy or assistant headteachers, and 22,090 headteachers.

- White British people accounted for 92.7 per cent of headteachers, 89.8 per cent of deputy or assistant headteachers and 85.2 per cent of classroom teachers (out of those whose ethnicity was known).

- White people of all backgrounds accounted for 91.9 per cent of classroom teachers.

- 0.1 per cent of classroom teachers were Mixed White and Black African, the lowest percentage out of all ethnic groups in this role.

- 0.1 per cent of deputy and assistant headteachers were from Mixed White, Black African, and Chinese ethnic groups, the lowest percentage of all ethnic groups in this role.

- In every type of school, teachers were least likely to be from Chinese or Mixed White and Black African ethnic groups.

Source: Department for Education (2021a)

The regional data paints much the same picture as the national data, even in culturally diverse areas such as my home city of Bristol. In 2018, while presenting a documentary for *BBC Inside Out West* with Tom Bigwood, I discovered that just 4.4 per cent of teachers in Bristol schools are from Black, Asian and minority ethnic backgrounds. The idea behind this documentary was born from the Runnymede Trust report of 2017, which found that Bristol was a divided city. The data was analysed further to look specifically at the number of Black teachers in state secondary schools in Bristol. The results concluded that:

- There were 26 Black teachers out of 1,346 (1.9 per cent).
- Nine out of the 19 state secondary schools in Bristol did not have any Black teachers.

Yet Black, Asian and minority ethnic children make up 33.6 per cent of the population in England (Department for Education, 2021b).

Lived experience: Jason Clarkson, head of year

In 2012, I was put forward by the school I worked in for what was referred to as a 'Black and Minority Ethnic (BME) leadership programme'. The apparent aim of this piece of work was to tackle the lack of diversity in middle and senior leadership in education. There were two sessions where the group was brought together and an opportunity to shadow colleagues at an educational setting that was recognised for the diversity of their leadership team.

I took the opportunity to spend a week at an inner-city secondary school in Birmingham, led by a Black headteacher. At that time, I had never met a Black headteacher before; I'd known some Black, Asian and minority ethnic teachers within education, or the occasional senior leader, but never a headteacher. This headteacher was also supported by a senior leadership team that included three 'BAME' practitioners.

This school was a larger-than-average secondary school, recognised for its population of students from minority ethnic backgrounds being well above the national average (Ofsted, 2011). The school was also located in the middle of a densely populated and low-income residential area, in which most of these students lived.

As a professional coming from an inner-city school in the south-west of England into this Midlands secondary school, I enjoyed many similarities in students' attitudes, personalities and energy. The schools local to me had White British headship and almost entirely White senior leadership teams. I thought it was amazing to meet this diverse leadership team, but when you spoke to the students they were not as impressed by it because to them it was 'normal'. As underwhelming as this seemed to me, comparing this Midlands school in 2012 to my schooling experience in the 1990s to mid-2000s, I now realise how fascinating and exceptional it was that those children had accepted that staffing demographic as their normal. While for me and some of my peers when we were younger, the thought of a Black headteacher may have seemed unimaginable, these young people experienced this every day.

What a young person experiences every day is their 'normal'; this impacts their dreams, aspirations and perceptions of what is realistic, likely or achievable. 'In a nutshell, students cannot be what they cannot see' (Mann et al., 2020).

In 2018, the lack of Black teachers became a big topic of conversation, particularly in Bristol (BBC News, 2018). Having worked in education for more than a decade, I can say that being a member of staff within a school was never in my plans as a young Black man. I had encouragement from some of my teachers telling me that I would be OK working in a school, but I didn't take them seriously.

I met two Caribbean men during my time in secondary school who helped shape me and my career choices. Being identified as 'BAME', my school had put me forward for a group for young 'BME' boys. This group meant I had access to a mentor I would talk to regularly. The other Caribbean man was a teaching assistant in some of my classes; we would sometimes end up in conversation during or after class, where he would always take the opportunity to impress some of his wisdom on me and some of my friends if ever there was the opportunity. Whenever I questioned what my teachers had said and that the thought of me working in a school was unrealistic, as I thought I would work in a bank and make loads of money, these men would always challenge me and ask me, 'Why?' They would always encourage me to express my opinions and beliefs. Still, both of these men forced me to question the limitation and think about why I could not work in a school or in any career for that matter. It turns out there was no reason why I could not, and now I have over a decade's worth of working in schools under my belt. It was role models such as these men who helped me see working in education as an option.

Having identifiable role models within a school is essential for our children. I always try to be the adult I needed when I was at school for the young people I work with today. In recent times, I have realised the significance of my skin and heritage and the inevitable experiences I will share with the people I work with. In the grand scheme of things I am not extraordinary; I now acknowledge that what I can do is very special. I have the potential to inspire any and every young person I come across. But, more expansive than my singular contributions to schools in the south-west of England, what can we do as a society to ensure every child has access to role models who will inspire and challenge them to a new normal? The thought of seeing a Black headteacher does not have to be an 'imagine if...' statement.

How many young people do you think we inspire every day without realising? What should we do to ensure that we are opening young Black, Asian and minority ethnic students to opportunities and experiences they wouldn't have thought possible? What can we do to help shape and mould our young people to recognise the power of their skin, culture or heritage as they grow into role models to those around them? How do we ensure that we encourage our young people to question their own perceptions of what is not achievable? What Black, Asian and minority ethnic role models are our young people missing and what can we do to make sure we fill those gaps with the right people?

Jason Clarkson is a head of year who specialises in pastoral and behavioural support for students aged 11–16 years old. As a White and Black Mixed Caribbean man, he advocates for the invisible child, ensuring they are heard.

Analysing the data in your school

It's essential to review the data in your own school to get a sense of where you are on your journey towards representation. How many of your school staff members are from a minoritised background? How does this compare with the number of pupils from these backgrounds in your school? Do you think your school staff body is representative of the children in your setting? Are any particular groups underrepresented or overrepresented? Collect the data carefully, draw some conclusions and think about what effect this might be having on the experiences pupils, staff, parents and carers have in your school. Here is some more information about the process of data collection to support you with this. I am grateful to school principal Ben Tucker for sharing his expertise in this section.

Data is defined as facts or figures which we can then use to make informed decisions within our organisations. In schools we want good data that provides indisputable evidence that allows us to identify potential issues, determine what we need to do next and to monitor and evaluate the effectiveness of the strategies we have put in place. As soon as any student or adult enters a school to learn or work, we start to collect data and importantly, data about protected characteristics. This includes age, disability, gender reassignment, race, religion or belief, sex, pregnancy and maternity, marriage and civil partnership. We can then use this data to consider our diversity and inclusion.

Data from students can show how diverse your school population is. Does your staff body represent your student population? Is your leadership team as diverse as your lower-paid employees? Data will answer these questions but it will not provide you with the solutions. Once you have considered the strategy that you are going to put in place, data can then be used to measure its effectiveness.

Attendance, attainment and progress data can be used alongside protected characteristics to consider how inclusive a school is. Again, the data will be able to answer questions such as how a specific group of students attends or performs in exams. Is this a trend that can be seen across several years? You will need to consider why this is the case and what you can do about it. You need to be aware of the size and validity of the group of students. If you only have two students in a specific group, this may not be the best indicator of performance.

Data is useful information that should be used as a helpful tool to consider how diverse and inclusive your organisation is, as long as it is collected and analysed with care.

Best practice for administrators involved in data collection

School administrators often provide support with the collection of data, so their help can be sought during this process. In this section, I am grateful to Gemma Cottle, a school data administrator, for providing some best practice for administrators involved in data collection.

When working with someone who produces data, an administrator would need to do the following things:

1. Find out exactly what the expectations are and what timeline you are working towards.

2. Ensure you are completely clear on how the data needs to be presented and what audience it is intended for.

3. Use conditional formatting or tables to ensure the results of the data can be easily identified.

It is always important to have clear and concise instructions from the manager on what it is they specifically need and then you can present the data in the way you feel is appropriate. Put forward ideas to a manager as to what you can contribute to ensuring the data is well presented. People have different skill sets and managers might not necessarily know about the tools that are available to present the data as clearly as possible. If you are recording subject choices, for example, you can populate a drop-down list for someone to choose options (rather than writing out the choices each time). You can then populate a formula in a cell called "COUNTIF", which will tell you how many times that option has been selected and therefore give you a running total. As an administrator, you may have more efficient and effective ways of doing things, as you have more experience. Never feel that you can't communicate this to senior members of the team, as they are generally extremely receptive to ideas from a specialist in the field.

Will hiring more diverse staff solve the issue?

Diversity is an interesting word; many interpretations and definitions of diversity can be drawn upon. It has become synonymous with ethnic diversity in recent years. But diversity is more than that. Hiring a few Black or Asian employees will solve your issues of 'diversity'. However, it certainly will not address racism or be enough to demonstrate anti-racist practice. In reality, it will achieve nothing more than providing a visual tick box.

Diversity can be defined as a collective of individuals who bring various views, opinions, experiences, perspectives, backgrounds, funds of knowledge, and parent or carer capital – those providing an asset to the setting. However, diversity should not be considered in isolation. It should be viewed in the context of equality, inclusion and belonging. Diversity in itself will not guarantee inclusivity.

Inclusion requires an organisation to use the ideas, skills and talents that all their staff have to offer, for the mutual benefit of the staff and students in the school. It also requires conscious thought and commitment from all stakeholders at all levels. It must involve the alignment of policies, procedures, curriculum content, school improvement plans and the behaviour of individuals.

Activity: The party analogy

The following is a well-known analogy to describe the differences between equality, diversity, inclusion and belonging. The original source of the analogy is unknown.

- Equality is the planning committee.
- Diversity is being invited to the party.
- Inclusion is being invited to dance.
- Belonging is choosing a song.

In your setting, who gets to contribute to the plan? Who is sitting at the table? Is anyone being left behind?

Valuing diversity and inclusion is not only morally and ethically right, but it also makes sense in any organisation. There should be diversity of thought in your classrooms, in your senior leadership meetings, in your lessons and on your boards. Suppose schools genuinely want to improve their diversity and inclusion practices. In that case, leaders must look beyond themselves and learn from the experiences of all their staff and students. This is how true change can take place. Only at this point can all stakeholders feel a sense of value and connection. This is how we create a legacy.

Analysing and reporting on data, and setting quotas and targets for a more diverse school workforce alongside holding hiring managers to account for meeting these targets, will improve diversity, but this compliance only serves to build an initial foundation for the more in-depth work required to achieve inclusivity. The World Economic Forum (2019) recommends organisations create a culture of diversity and inclusion that is 'infused in every aspect' of the organisation, from recruitment and reward to talent and performance management. Further to this, there must be a focus on changing behaviours, attitudes and mindsets. They summarise this approach in three stages. I have added some advice for schools for each stage.

1. 'Diversity for compliance': This serves only to create a 'foundational culture' of diversity and inclusion.

   Advice for schools: It is important to ensure that you are not simply focused on visual diversity and pooling recruitment at the grassroots levels. Ensure that there is ethnic diversity at all levels. What recruitment, retention and promotion opportunities are being provided?

2. 'Specific policies': Diversity and inclusion are 'integrated into recruitment, rewards, talent management and performance management'.

   Advice for schools: All policies should receive an equality impact assessment. The voices of the most marginalised should be sought and considered in relation to these policies. Where is the impact of these policies being felt the most?

3. 'Targets and quotas': Targets are combined with a focus on changing culture and mindsets within the organisation.

   Advice for schools: Targets in isolation can be tokenistic. However, in conjunction with other initiatives, targets can be a great source of inspiration and accountability. They can be used as a baseline for the future and to measure progress.

What else needs to be considered besides the data?

If the diversity of the school workforce is only one piece of the puzzle to achieve inclusivity, what other aspects of your school need to be reviewed at this stage of your journey? Take an objective look at the following through the lens of race and representation. Be honest: do they promote equality? Do they represent the diversity of your school community? Do they show an inclusive environment? Do they make pupils, parents, carers, staff and all other stakeholders feel that they belong in your setting?

- **The school website:** the information being provided, the branding of the school, the images being displayed and the language being used.
- **The physical environment:** the entrance hall, classrooms, corridors, playground, display boards and all other spaces.
- **The resources:** those you are using in the classroom with pupils and those you send home to parents and carers for home-learning.
- **The training:** CPD and any other training courses your school staff have undertaken in the past and are currently undertaking.
- **The objectives, policies and procedures:** what do you currently have in place for equity, diversity and inclusion? Do you have anti-racist policies? Do you have a specific policy that addresses behaviour? Does your safeguarding policy take into account racism, microaggressions and intersectionality? Do you already have an action plan or a strategy? Does the work you're doing relate to your values?

It's also important to consult with staff, students, governors and the wider school community and understand their perspectives on the school. Ask them what they think about all of the above aspects of your school and how they feel more generally about the setting. Do they feel they belong? Do they feel represented, seen and heard? Listen to stakeholders from all backgrounds, but focus on the marginalised voices. Have they had any experiences of discrimination or racism (either overt or covert) in your school? If so, were these incidents dealt with appropriately or could additional support have been provided? Example questions would be:

1. Have you ever felt excluded from workplace activities or opportunities based on your ability, race, sex or background?
2. 'I feel people in leadership roles have encouraged my development within my workplace?' Do you agree or disagree with this statement?

3. What does our workplace do well regarding equity, diversity and inclusion?

4. What changes could be made in our school culture to make it more inclusive?

Use focus groups and listening circles to facilitate discussion. It might be helpful to ask a third party to lead on this, as they can report back objectively, and staff, students and parents may feel they can be more open and honest. Utilise the information to highlight trends, issues and gaps in knowledge. The aim is to lift the lid and review all aspects of your setting.

Throughout this process, it is important to listen carefully and objectively and take on board all that is being shared. Be sensitive: these conversations are not easy, particularly for those people who may be reliving their trauma by speaking about incidents that have impacted them. It is imperative that you do not get defensive or try to deny their lived experience. Instead, express your gratitude to them for sharing their experiences with you, take detailed notes and pledge to hold yourself accountable to bring about positive change.

Part 2 of this book will go into more detail about how to facilitate conversations about race and racism in a school setting.

Lived experience: Bianca Williams, deputy director of sixth form

Racism: a foreign concept for some and a regular experience for others. As I reflect on my educational journey, I vividly remember a string of racist encounters, each memory automatically evoking feelings of both sadness and disappointment that will forever stay with me. Not only did my experiences of racism shape me as an educator, but they also led me into the teaching profession – hopeful that I could be part of the drive for positive change as well as the visible representation that I longed to see as a young, impressionable Black female student.

My primary school studies began in the nineties, in an area of London that was very much diverse and inclusive of all ethnicities and cultures. Each month in my primary school, we would celebrate the various cultures that comprised our school. I look back at these times with deep fondness, as it was during these years that I truly felt a strong sense of belonging. Little did I know that this would be the last time I would feel as though I really belonged as a student within an educational setting.

Having attended that primary school for a few years, my family announced that they would be relocating to a different area of London, which meant that I would have to change primary school. At the time I felt excited at the prospect of moving into a bigger house, going to a new school and meeting new friends. However, this excitement came to be short-lived.

My first day at my new school arrived. My hair had been freshly braided, with red bobbles that matched my uniform for an added touch, and my patent black shoes were fresh out of the box. My crisp uniform was reflective of my eagerness to learn, explore and expand my friendship group. I was more than ready for what I imagined would be a great first day.

As I was given a tour of my new school with my parents in tow, I very quickly realised that the school was a stark contrast to what I had been used to. I came to realise that I was the only minority ethnic student – let alone Black student – in my entire year group. In spite of this, I remained hopeful that my new school incorporated similar values and attitudes to diversity that I had been used to in my previous school. I did not let the lack of diversity impact the goals I had set to achieve that day.

I was quickly settled into my class group by one of the teaching assistants. Once my parents felt satisfied that I had successfully settled among my new peers, they sauntered off into the school corridors, not to be seen again until the end of the school day. I remember being 'buddied up' with a student who was told to show me the ropes and to introduce me to my fellow peers. What I had thought to be a pleasant introduction quickly escalated into what I would know to be a nightmare for years to come.

A helicopter flew above the playground and I was immediately met with chants that the helicopter was full of police who were coming to take me back to Africa. Incidentally I am of Caribbean heritage, but I digress. I felt humiliated, alienated, and longed to go back to my previous school where diversity was celebrated. As I approached the dinner ladies to explain what had happened, I was met with bouts of laughter and a synchronised, 'I'm sure they were only playing with you!' There was no attempt to resolve the issue and I went home deflated. They completely dismissed my experience, and further added to my already intense feelings of not belonging.

At the end of the school day, my parents greeted me at the school gate, both equally eager to hear about the proceedings of my first day. My facial expression gave it all away. Whilst I had hoped to downplay the events of my day in a bid not to concern my parents, my face simply said it all. Having explained what had happened, they agreed that they would speak with my teachers if it were to happen again.

Days later, there was little improvement and I dreaded going into school. On this one particular day, I had chosen to wear a Disney watch that I had been gifted for my birthday. It was a liquid water watch that I had hoped would be sufficient enough to keep me occupied during play time. It soon attracted those very peers who were at the centre of my disdain. Keen to let bygones be bygones, I was allured into letting one of the students try my watch on. I had hoped that they had experienced a change of heart and were now keen to get to know who I was beyond my skin colour. This naivety, I soon realised, would be to my own detriment. One of those students very quickly threw my watch to the ground and stomped on it. As I frantically went to pick up my watch, all that remained was broken glass and leaked water – the perfect metaphor for how I felt at that very moment. Crushed.

Just as I thought this moment couldn't get any worse, a loud aeroplane flew over the playground and lo and behold the 'Go back to Africa!' chants started. I immediately alerted the dinner ladies again, and as expected I was met with laughter and dismissal. They even went as far as to say my watch had probably been broken long before I'd let the other student wear it. My eyes welled with tears. I felt powerless, violated and angry. Eager to take this further, I was sure to explain every detail of my experience to my parents that very afternoon. Disgusted and appalled, they arranged a meeting with my school teacher that very same day. It was later agreed that my dad would come into my class to talk about racism and why it should not be tolerated. In hindsight, I am still confused as to why that important lesson had been placed on my father to deliver, as opposed to a teacher at the school. However, at the time I was young and just happy that something was being done about the abuse that I'd experienced.

Whilst I can confidently say my dad's visit had some impact, the racism still remained. Only now it was much more implicit and covert. It could be as simple as being the last person to be picked for a team in physical education, or notes being passed around suggesting my skin colour looked like poo. I continued to rise above it all, pledging that I would do my best to challenge racism.

In my adult years, I have come to realise that it is an even bigger issue than I'd thought. The racism that I experience now is even more subtle, embedded within the very institutions that are supposed to educate and liberate.

It is important to remember that the most diverse companies have the most successes, and that is not a coincidence. Diversity needs to be celebrated, not tolerated.

Bianca Williams is a deputy director of sixth form and a teacher of psychology in her seventh year of teaching. She teaches in a mixed-comprehensive secondary school situated in London.

Equality versus equity

Diversity and inclusion have become a billion-dollar industry. But the reality is that often the most marginalised do not benefit from the work, as we are still stuck in the hamster wheel of believing that equality is enough.

Equality is simple. It means giving everyone the same. But the same equality that we seek to use as a tool of fairness can become a tool of oppression. For example, providing stairs may present as equal access to a building. After all, everyone is entitled to use them. We would all agree that this is ludicrous. Wheelchair users would not be able to use the stairs and therefore would not have equal access to the building. Providing a lift or a ramp would be more equitable. We adjust the support required based on the needs of a particular group of people. Yet, when we consider this in the context of race, we often return to deficit and 'whataboutery'. If we give people from a particular ethnic group support based on their specific needs, we will hear someone ask, 'But what about…?' This has to stop. One of the purposes of collecting and analysing data about particular ethnic groups and their experiences of education is to identify their specific needs and to devise a plan to support them. We will only be able to do this by collecting granular data through a very specific lens. Collecting data on 'BAME' communities is not good enough. Each of the communities covered by the acronym 'BAME' will have their own experiences and their own specific needs.

While aiming for equity over equality is a step in the right direction, it will only get us so far. We need not just equity, but justice and liberation. The question is, do we all get the opportunity to experience this? It is argued that we live in a diverse society and that we all have access to the same opportunities. The reality is that we do not all start from the same place. We may all have equal opportunities, but the access to these opportunities comes with barriers. We need to move away from equality, exchange it for equity and think about freeing all communities to be the best version of themselves.

Adapted from IISC (interactioninstitute.org) and artist Angus Maguire along with the original concept image from Craig Froehle (2016).

Summary

Key learning points

- When it comes to data, language is important. The language you use can skew the results you receive. Before collecting and analysing data, think about which lens you are using. What is it that you want to know? Then when you know, what will you do about it? Which of the following lenses will you use to capture data and how might they skew your results?

  - Black
  - Asian
  - South Asian
  - East and South-East Asian
  - BAME (Black, Asian and minority ethnic)
  - BME (Black and minority ethnic)
  - VME (visual minority ethnic)
  - BIPOC (Black, Indigenous and People of Colour)
  - POC (People of Colour)
  - Mixed heritage

  Should we still be using BAME to describe communities, particularly when considering data?

- Diversity and inclusion are not the same thing. Hiring more staff from ethnic minority backgrounds will improve diversity but to achieve inclusion there must be a focus on changing behaviours, attitudes and mindsets.

- To get started on this journey, complete an objective audit of your school. Think about the school website, the physical environment, the resources you're using, staff CPD and your current policies for diversity, equity and inclusion. Consult with pupils, parents, staff and other key stakeholders, invite their opinions and listen to their lived experiences.

Key question

How often do you think about diversity?

a) Every time I walk into a room.

b) When I see it in the media.

c) When it is an agenda item.

d) Hardly ever.

Your answer to the above will probably depend on whether this is your lived experience. I know that when I walk into a room, my first thought is: am I the only Black woman in the room? How psychologically safe am I going to be? For others, it may not be a concern or a thought that they ever need to grapple with beyond an obligatory training session at the beginning of the academic year.

Further self-reflection questions

1. How do you actively celebrate diversity within your workplace setting?
2. Does the leadership team within your workplace reflect the diversity that exists within your staff or student body?
3. How can you tackle racism within your workplace or school setting?

Discussion points for staff meetings

- Think about data. Does it matter to you? Does it matter that the school's leadership team does not reflect its support staff? When you see a lack of diversity, do you respond to the needs of your school community or are you hesitant to respond?
- If your setting is not diverse, and most staff and students aren't minoritised, can you skip the debate and go on to the next chapter?

PART 2

Listening and decentring

3 Should we talk to children about race?

'There is no such thing as race. None. There is just a human race – scientifically and anthropologically.'

Toni Morrison

In an ideal world, there would be no need to have a conversation with my children about race – certainly not in the context of racial segregation and racism. However, it's become quite apparent that if I didn't have this conversation with my children, I would be failing them. I'd be raising ill-prepared children, not ready for a world they'll almost certainly have to navigate in the future. They'd be raised with the false belief that the world is equal and fair and that their race would never be a barrier for them. The reality is that racial superiority exists. It is real and manifests itself in all aspects of society, including education.

Children notice race irrespective of whether adults see it or initiate the conversation. Therefore, our responsibility is to provide context, understanding, language and tools that will support and equip our children to have conversations about race and racism. Whether we have these conversations with our children or decide to ignore this crucial issue, children will continue to formulate their own ideas and understanding.

When we as adults claim that we do not see race, when we say that we are 'colour-blind', it's a microinvalidation. Our children are not transparent. We see the different shades of skin, we see the beautiful colour hues, we see the different hair textures, we see the cultural differences. We see them. But it is easier to pretend that we do not. By doing this we are causing serious and lasting harm. We cannot ignore who our children are. If we do that, we centre Whiteness and perpetuate the ideology that Whiteness equals normality. (It's important to note that not only is the justification of being 'colour-blind' problematic for People of Colour, but the word itself is also problematic as an ableist term that equates blindness with ignorance. 'Colour-evasiveness' has been suggested as a possible alternative (Annamma et al., 2017).)

In my 2019 TEDx Talk, I said:

'We play into the hands of racial hierarchy, bias and representative oppression, because those are the cards we have been dealt. But imagine a world where you are taught the value of all races. Racial superiority is stripped of its crown, and instead, all races are treated with equal importance. Children will grow with a sense of value, connection and understanding of difference.'

For future generations of children, my hope and vision is that we can teach the value and importance of who we all are, irrespective of race. But for now, the conversation regarding race and racism must continue to happen. Children must be taught about this, and schools have their part to play.

Having 'the talk'

Our hesitation and reluctance to speak to children about race are a reflection of our own discomfort. We project our fears onto them and, in doing so, prevent the opportunity for growth and connection. We need to stop and take stock of our own core beliefs and understanding of the world. We need to question why it makes us feel uncomfortable. We need to pause, reflect and question the knot in our stomach, our sweaty palms, our pounding heart. Our body screams at us that it does not want to do it, so we succumb to the physical feelings and convince our conscious mind that our children are not ready. The truth is that it is us who aren't prepared, not them.

When born, babies look at all races in the same way. At three months, they can look at faces and match them to their parents or carers. By the age of two, they are using race to reason and make decisions about the behaviours of other children. Yet it's often left until later in their educational journey – or until an incident occurs – before children are allowed to have these discussions.

Silence reinforces racism. We must have these discussions to progress and make sustainable and long-lasting change for the next generation. This is more than equality. We are talking about equity. This is a need.

I recently sat with a friend and colleague and asked her a simple question: have you ever *talked*? She quickly said, 'Yeah, about boys and sex.' I said, 'No, about race.' She looked at me somewhat confused. If you are racialised as White, you would naturally think I'm talking about sex. However, for parents of Black children, 'the talk' is a very different conversation. It's not about the birds and the bees, rather a discussion about life and death. As a parent, I never wanted to have 'the chat'. It was certainly not a talk I was looking forward to. Yet I knew that as a parent of two Black boys, I had no choice. How could I not talk to my sons about race? How could I not inform them of the negativity that would be put upon them? It's not something I could avoid.

My son was due to start secondary school and I would no longer take him to and from school. It was time for him to be independent. Why was my heart pounding? It wasn't because I was worried that he would be hit by a car or because my baby was growing up. I was worried about him being attacked on the street because of his skin. I was concerned about the first time the police would stop him. And to be clear, it was not an 'if', it was a 'when'.

We sat down in our living room. I remember the light shining through the window. I could see the sun glistening and reflecting against his beautiful brown eyes. His pupils were large and dilated; he was fearful. What was Mummy going to say? Little did he know what I was thinking: when did society decide that my beautiful baby had become a threat? A threat because he was growing up to become a Black man.

Less than a year after the chat, it happened. He came home and said, 'Mummy, Mummy, it happened.' I remember looking him up and down, checking him over, searching for any sign of harm. But he looked fine. I said, 'What happened?' He explained that he was walking from the train station when a White female police officer approached him and asked him his name and where he was going. He said, 'Mummy, I responded politely. I responded with my name and asked if I could unzip my coat.' He explained that he was on his way to school and she let him go. I then asked him if she'd stopped anyone else. He said, 'No, she only stopped me but there were other people around.'

I breathed a sigh of relief that he was OK. But I knew this would not be his last stop and search experience.

There is a global perspective around the issue of threat and suspicion. While it's regularly denied, the fact is that at a structural and institutional level, Black skin is seen as threatening. This affects your students, and it manifests itself in your behaviour policies. This is clear from the data regarding disproportionate exclusions and the number of Black and Asian students in custody. Black children in particular are often adultified: instead of being considered children or teenagers, they are treated like adults due to a perceived 'threat'. How does a child avoid looking suspicious and threatening?

Question

At what point in a child's life do they become a 'threat' and how does this impact on the educational experience they have?

Should we challenge racist behaviour in children?

When my eldest son started primary school, he attended a school with a mostly White British demographic. It wasn't local; it was a short distance from our home. I chose it because they had a good Ofsted rating, and the right things were said when we looked around. I felt safe; he felt safe. Within a term of him starting, a racially motivated incident occurred. He was chased, stamped on and rubbed in mud. Then two children stood on his hands, coat and school work. It breaks my heart when I replay in my mind the damage that this has caused to my son.

He was four; the children were four. I brought it to the attention of the headteacher. The school was as supportive as they felt they could be. But it was not good enough. My child was unsafe. He was under attack because of his skin.

Who should I have been upset with? The four-year-old who had been taught to dislike children who looked like my son? The school? The children were in Reception… apparently not ready to talk about race and identity. The parents? I believe they played a part. This behaviour was taught at home. Those children's sources of knowledge were clear to see. But ultimately, you have to start with society: the system, the structure.

I often talk to educators about the power and privilege that they hold. We have an opportunity to challenge the ideologies taught to our children. We have the opportunity to talk about their belief systems and the prejudicial ideas that they hold. We may be the only people who challenge our children's perspective and understanding. But we need to be intentional about this. We must be intentional about anti-racist practice. It must include our children, and it must be woven into all aspects of education.

Activity: The four dimensions of racism

There are four dimensions of racism:

1. **Structural:** This occurs where multiple institutions uphold racism.
2. **Institutional:** This can manifest itself in policies and practices that reinforce racist standards within a workplace.
3. **Interpersonal:** This is the relationship between people. It includes racist acts and microaggressions carried out from person to person.

4. Individual or internalised: This addresses the individual. Internalised core beliefs and bias lead to subtle and overt messages that reinforce negative beliefs and self-hatred.

Complete the triangle: how do these four dimensions of racism manifest themselves in education?

We often hear educators and teachers challenge the age that discussions about racism begin, with comments such as, 'You are teaching the children to be racist' or 'You are putting thoughts into their head.' In reality, children as young as 18 months can identify races and by the age of three to five, they will already be developing racial bias (Aboud, 2008).

Children might make comments such as, 'Are you made of chocolate?' or 'You cannot come to my party; we are not allowed Black people at our house' or 'Your hair is not nice hair like mine.' These types of comments are often dismissed or shrugged off – on the basis that the child didn't mean it or didn't understand what they were saying. But what happens if we leave these comments? What if they remain unchecked and are not challenged or addressed? Do these children become the very adults whom we are challenging now and asking to address their racist practices and ideas?

While we often look to the parents or carers as the parties to blame for childhood racist ideas, ideologies can also be compounded by other cultural and societal norms that reinforce a racial superiority complex (Hirschfeld, 2008). Children may recognise race and form ideas that all people of a similar skin are the same and have the same skills and attributes, as we see in the 'doll test' (see page 55). This extends further for our children. They may see people of a particular skin colour working in a certain job and begin to define that job by racial group. For example, children might believe all police staff are White. The next logical conclusion could easily be that they believe all authority figures are – and should be – White. This is how children learn to attach meaning to race without an adult explicitly giving them these ideas. We also see this in popular culture. What happens if you ask a young child to describe a prince and princess? Racial cues and gender stereotypes are likely to be present, as that will often be the depiction that they have seen or encountered. Would a Black child ever imagine they could be a prince or princess?

Both consciously and unconsciously, the standards of Whiteness, as a culture and an ideology (see page 86), are given to children as the bar that they need to attain. It is the standard that needs to be reached. If we are to challenge this, we need to educate our children intentionally and directly about the construct of race and how it manifests in society. Education will play a vital role in these building blocks. As Aristotle said, 'Give me a child until he is seven and I will show you the man.' Whilst this quote may be argued to be gender exclusive, the sentiment is clear. What we teach our children today will determine who they are tomorrow. In the following lived experience piece, Early Years specialist Shaddai Tembo offers some theory and practice to support educators in teaching young children about racism.

Lived experience: Shaddai Tembo, Early Years lecturer, writer and speaker

The racism that we experience as adults in society finds its feet in the Early Years of our lives. This section will initially consider the importance of early childhood as a formative stage, before examining intersections with race through the ways in which children begin to become attentive to difference. From here, I will apply an equalities perspective to consider how issues around racism can begin to emerge, both from adults and between children themselves. The final section will consider some aspects of an anti-racist approach and examine how we might better support all children to recognise and challenge racism in the Early Years.

The importance of the Early Years

We have long known from many different perspectives about the significance of the Early Years, both in our overall development and more specifically in the formation of our identities. Contemporary advances in the field of neuroscience, however, provide the most striking case for taking early childhood seriously. While we never truly stop developing new connections within our cognitive architectures, research over the past two decades has emphasised the ways in which the first few years of our lives are especially sensitive periods during which an extraordinary amount of discovery takes place. Experiences here can have a long-term effect on the rest of children's lives in terms of shaping their learning and allowing them to reach their potential.

Just as importantly, neuroscientific knowledge has come to call time on the weary 'nature versus nurture debate', the ongoing contention that our development is wholly determined by either our genetic makeup (the nature argument) or through social factors (the nurture argument). We have, as Gina Rippon (2019) describes, 'social brains'. As she explains:

> 'In today's understanding of the brain we are appreciating more and more that what our brain does with our world very much depends on the information it has extracted from that world… if the information it soaks up is biased in some way, perhaps based on prejudice and stereotypes, then it is not hard to see what the outcome might be.'

Recognising the social nature of our brains matters. This allows us to consider the broader role of the environment in shaping our individual early selves, including our families, our cultural and community context, as well as our broader attitudes, beliefs and customs. In recognising this we are able to challenge an idealised, somewhat utopian, image of childhood as a period in our lives that is seemingly free from broader societal issues. Rippon goes on to make a compelling argument for the influence of stereotypical beliefs around gender in shaping our identities from birth, while here I intend to follow others in making a similar case for children's early perceptions of difference and the role of race. Just as we are gendered from birth, we are implicated in a racialised world too.

Becoming attentive to difference

Consciously or not, from birth, children begin to develop an understanding about others on the basis of how they look and the colour of their skin. Research has shown that even by the time they are three months old, babies tend to look longer at faces from their own racial group or familiar racial groups compared to faces from other, less familiar racial groups (Kelly et al., 2005). This differentiation only increases with age, so by around two years old children will begin to use those markers to classify social groups and to identify themselves as part of their own ongoing identity formation. Further studies have shown that by three and four years old, children of all races tend to hold pro-White biases that can lead to racialised preferences in terms of friendship and for resources (MacNevin and Berman, 2016; Naughton and Davis, 2009). Together, these studies clearly demonstrate how children in the Early Years can internalise social norms around race. Of course, if we are to take equalities seriously and address racism in educational contexts and wider society, these social norms must be recognised and challenged. A position of silence, where educators find it too uncomfortable to discuss these issues, or a so-called 'colour-blind' attitude, where educators treat all children the same and homogenise difference, will only perpetuate racism against Black, Asian and minoritised children.

Racism in the nursery

My own experience as an Early Years practitioner reminds me of many conversations during play with children when the topic of skin colour would come up. As one of few visibly non-White practitioners, I know all too well about the inquisitive nature of children when it comes to difference. More often than not, these questions and comments were entirely innocent. They provided an opportunity to speak openly and allowed children to develop ideas about others that were not solely informed by the stereotypical depictions that they had encountered elsewhere. Yet I suspect I was the exception that proves the rule: as a profession we are still not doing enough to challenge the existence of racism in the Early Years. To illustrate this on a more systematic level, we can turn to the Early Years Foundation Stage Profile (EYFSP) teacher assessments. These are intended to support practitioners in making accurate judgements about each child's attainment. However, it seems clear that there is already a level of racism at play. In nearly every year since 2013, Black children have been assessed as the lowest-achieving overall ethnicity group (Department for Education, 2019). Either we fall back on the side of nature to explain this – that there is a genetic basis for achievement – or we recognise that racism permeates all aspects of a child's life, from their developing ideas about themselves through to how their level of development is assessed by others. While this is a multifaceted issue, these assessments in the Early Years must be recognised as part of the longer pipeline through which educational contexts continue to perpetuate racism (Wallace and Joseph-Salisbury, 2021).

What can be done in Early Years settings?

So far, I have emphasised the importance of the Early Years of our lives and also considered how our heavily racialised society can affect children's perceptions of themselves and others. This section will consider some aspects of an anti-racist approach that can be developed within your settings to enhance practice. This will not be an extensive list. Nor is it intended as a checklist for you to tick off (as if racism could be solved that way), rather the intention is that you think through some of these points and adapt them to your own individual contexts. Importantly, this work should be ongoing, in the same way you do your daily risk assessments. There is no reason why you cannot reflect on your approach toward equalities on a fortnightly or monthly basis.

1. Agree on a strategy

As part of your wider equalities strategy or policy informed by the Equality Act 2010, you should aim to have a specific and ongoing focus on anti-racism. This requires a 'whole-setting' approach where all staff have the opportunity to comment, share their views and commit to the actions you put forward. This is a really good opportunity to have these kinds of discussions, which is why parents and carers should also have the chance to comment. This document should be freely available for all to see, including new parents and new members of staff, and could also include some contributions from the children themselves.

2. Check your environment

Carry out an equalities check on your nursery environment and answer the following quick questions:

- Is there anything that reinforces racial stereotypes?
- Is there anything that challenges racial stereotypes?
  - ◦ Think about your literacy area and books.
  - ◦ Think about your resources.
  - ◦ Think about your material displays.

These questions are only a loose guide and can be built upon as you continue to expand your own knowledge about how to promote anti-racist practice. Wherever possible, you should aim for resources that reflect the cultural make-up of your children and their communities. Resources from cultures that children might be unfamiliar with need to be introduced in a careful and respectful way. This is your opportunity to engage with the wider community and offer meaningful learning experiences for the child. It is also really important to note that it is as much about how adults can support children to engage in resources, as the resources themselves. It is all well and good to say that you have books featuring Black, Asian or other minoritised children, but if you are not actually reading these books on a regular basis in the same way as you would with more traditional (White) books, little is gained.

3. Think about intersectionality

Our lives are so much more complex than is often presented on paper. As mentioned on page 24, intersectionality is a concept originally coined by Black feminist Kimberlé Crenshaw, and formerly articulated by the Combahee River Collective, to address how differing aspects of our identities can shape the specific ways that we each experience inequality. This allows us to consider how race is inextricably interwoven with gender, class, sexuality, age, religion and ability. Crucially, it allows for a more accurate understanding of the complexities of children's lived experiences. Keeping intersectionality at the forefront of our thinking helps us understand how a child's experience of racism can be exacerbated through several other factors.

Shaddai Tembo is a lecturer in early childhood practice, a trustee for Early Education and the Fatherhood Institute, and an independent writer and speaker at Critical Early Years.

The role of representation in child development

'No one is born hating another person because of the colour of his skin, or his background, or his religion. People learn to hate, and if they can learn to hate, they can be taught to love, for love comes more naturally to the human heart than its opposite.'
Nelson Mandela (1994)

The issue of race begins at conception. It is not a choice. When it comes to talking to children about race, it cannot happen soon enough.

Asian women are twice as likely, and Black women four times as likely, to die during pregnancy or childbirth compared to White women (Knight et al., 2020). Therefore, before these children are out of their mother's womb, they are being subjected to structural racial inequalities that can prevent them from even accessing life.

I think often about the doll test created by husband-and-wife team Kenneth and Mamie Clark in the 1940s. They used the test to investigate how young Black children viewed their racial identities. While not surprising, their findings were still astonishing. Given the choice between Black dolls and White dolls, most Black children preferred to play with White dolls. When they were asked why, they were able to describe the White dolls from a very positive perspective, yet when describing the Black dolls, the descriptors were very negative. However, the part that I find most emotional upon reading and watching this experiment time and time again is the moment when the penny drops. When the children are asked which doll looks most like them. They then realise that the very doll that they had not liked, the doll they had rejected, the doll they had called ugly – that was the doll that looked most like them. Clark and Clark concluded in their findings that Black children see themselves in a negative light due to the racist society that they've been raised in.

My fear is for the children who are not raised to see the beauty in their own skin. How often are they being celebrated for who they are? As a Black mother who is always celebrating Black excellence and empowerment, I still had to process and digest the moment when my son said, 'Mummy, I don't want to be Black.' I remind him of this now and he says, 'I love being Black. Did I really say that?' But at the age of six – when you are being educated to believe that Blackness is not beautiful, when you are conditioned to feel that you are not good enough, when other children reject you because you are Black – I can understand why a Black child would develop self-hatred and anti-Blackness towards themselves. But what happens when this is not addressed?

I think of my niece who is currently three years of age. She is of dual heritage. Her father is a Black Caribbean descendant. Her mother is White British. She has two dolls that look the same in physical appearance. One has white skin with yellow hair. One has brown skin with dark brown hair. I find myself watching her play, just looking to see which doll she chooses to play with. I often wonder which doll she thinks she looks like more. Mostly, she waves the Black doll at me and says, 'Aunty, this is you!' Her parents are very keen for her to be raised in a way that allows her to celebrate all parts of her heritage and culture. However, I can't help but think: if she is racialised as Black, will she ever have the chance to understand both parts of her identity equally? Will her parents be preparing her adequately for life as a dual-heritage child, who will ultimately be racialised as Black, if they teach her that she gets to choose?

Part 1

Consider the following two photographs:

1. A woman stands at a dressing table. She is wearing an expensive jacket, skirt, red shirt and heels, and is adjusting her jewellery, getting ready to go out. A second woman is sitting on a couch next to her in a maid's uniform, breastfeeding a baby. The woman getting ready and the baby are racialised as Black. The maid is racialised as White. This photograph was taken by Julia Fullerton-Batten and you can see it on her website at: https://juliafullerton-batten.com/project/the-wet-nurse-2014.

2. A man sits on a doorstep holding a gun, dressed in a shirt, hat and trousers. A second man stands to the side, also holding a gun. Next to these men are four men chained together with a thick chain around their necks and hands. The man seated on the doorstep holds the end of the chain. The four men in chains are naked except for rags and are covered in dirt, wounds and scars. The men in chains are racialised as White. This photograph was taken by Greg Semu and you can see it on the CNN website at: https://edition.cnn.com/style/article/greg-semu-blood-red-australia/index.html.

Take a look at the photographs and think about the following questions:

- What thoughts and emotions come to mind?
- Would you be happy for your child to be raised seeing these images?
- These are the everyday experiences of Black, Brown and racially minoritised children. What does this do to their psyche?

Part 2

Bring to mind an image of a medical diagram that shows a pregnant woman with a baby growing in her womb. Consider these questions:

- What is the colour of the woman and baby's skin?
- What do their features look like?
- How would the woman and baby be racialised?

It is likely that the image you brought to mind was of a woman and baby who would be racialised as White by the colour of their skin and the representation of their features.

In 2021, an illustration by medical student Chidiebere Ibe went viral. It showed a Black baby in the womb of a Black woman. The image highlighted the lack of representation in illustrations in medical textbooks and scientific journals. You can view this image and more of Chidiebere's illustrations on his Instagram page: @ebereillustrate.

Take a look at some of Chidiebere's illustrations and think about the following questions:

- Why is it important that medical illustrations represent people from a wide range of ethnicities?
- What impact could these illustrations have for students if they were used in medical textbooks?
- Why are accuracy and authenticity important in these images?
- What can you take away from this for your own classroom practice? Think about the resources and activities you use to deliver and embed subject content for your students.

In a lesson at school, my son was asked to watch a video on YouTube about The Empire. The video did not have a trigger warning. A few moments later there were images of Black people standing in rows with chains around their necks. So many videos and programmes we watch today come with a warning about images and how they could affect you. Yet there was no warning for this. It made me wonder: why is this type of image not treated with the same trigger warning? The presenter in the video made an opening statement: 'The British had a moral duty to civilise these people.' My son's question followed: 'Mummy, did we need civilising?'

Question

What did this experience do to all the children of colour in this lesson? What did it reinforce to the White children?

In another lesson, my youngest son and his friend got into a verbal dispute with another child. She said to them, 'Go away, you slaves.' The boys explained to the teacher what had happened. Now I must provide context about why this is relevant. The Year 5 class were learning about Black history and the day before had been learning about slaves. What is interesting is this: for this young primary school child, in less than 24 hours, she'd learned the role Black people had played in society and had chosen to use it as a slur against the Black boys in the class.

Representation is crucial to the development of young children, as this instance may have been the only representation of Black people that this child had experienced. Her young brain is developing core beliefs and this lack of knowledge could have had a huge impact on her future value of Black boys in society. The sad truth is that this incident is not isolated – it is an experience that has been echoed for decades. Whilst I agree slavery and its atrocities should be taught, we must not neglect to tell the whole story.

In March 2021, the UK government released 'Commission on Race and Ethnic Disparities: The Report'. The report highlighted that there is no evidence of institutional racism in the UK and that the UK is a 'beacon' for race relations. The report effectively gaslighted the lived experiences of millions of people. The reality is that even when race is not a concern in the context of the discussion there is still a disproportionate impact on minority communities. Even if it is argued that the UK is not racist, it is extremely hard to deny the racism displayed in our everyday society. Let us take a moment to pause and reflect. We can see that where we are in society today is the result of a system founded upon principles that have promoted occupation, slavery, domination and genocide.

Education cannot escape this. It is a matter of safety.

Often conversations regarding race are deemed to be educational. Racism and prejudicial comments are considered a behaviour concern, although sometimes logged as a safeguarding concern. If you ask parents and carers for the top three things they expect from a school, the answers will often include the following: happiness, attainment and safety. All of which would be perfectly fair. But what if my child is not safe in school because of the colour of their skin? This could lead to verbal or physical abuse. It could lead to trauma or mental health concerns. It could lead to suicide ideation or death. Racism must be treated with the same level of concern as all other aspects of safeguarding. Safeguarding is everyone's responsibility and so is racism.

Teaching children as young as possible about the importance of celebrating difference in culture, whilst stamping out racism and making it clear it is wrong, keeps them safe and begins to change the rhetoric that has continued in education for years. Children are never too young to be taught about safety. The sooner they learn, the faster it is embedded.

Lived experience: Chantelle Douglas, Key Stage 1 teacher

My earliest memories surrounding my early years of education are closely tied to my identity and representation in general. The first memory is related to a lending library of books at my nursery and asking my mum why she had chosen a specific book. The book is *Eat Up, Gemma* by Sarah Hayes. Don't get me wrong – I loved this book (and still do!). When I asked my mum, she replied that she wanted to choose a book that had Black characters. The second memory revolved around me and my peer arguing over a Black baby doll – me insisting it was my go to have the baby doll and refusing to choose anything else to play with.

While these memories may seem very generic – nostalgic books and a favourite toy – they serve to show the importance of representation and seeing yourself. These are two of my clearest memories from that time (around three years old), and they don't have any obvious, overriding emotional connotations tied to them. I loved *Eat Up, Gemma* (and *Amazing Grace*, which was also borrowed a lot from nursery), and the only emotion in the baby doll memory is a sadness that it was not my turn. So, what is it about those memories that are so clear? I can only hazard a guess that they revolve around a part of my identity. Why were there only two books with Black characters, and why was it so important that I took them home? Why did I have the feeling that this was the only baby doll I wanted to play with?

As has been established, by the age of about three, children are more likely to seek out White playmates. You can only assume that this is because they may have possibly concluded that Whiteness is synonymous with being good or popular or nice. And to be fair, who can blame them? Education (as we know) is extremely underrepresented as a sector. I have spent time in a number of settings and have been either the only Black member of staff or one of fewer than a handful (none in the Early Years, where children's ideas around their identity are still being formed). I have been told by children that I was a Chinese dancer who had performed earlier that day or that their toys don't like me because I have brown skin. If all children are seeing is Whiteness, then it is not surprising that this will impact their ideas of race and identity. If the people within settings do not feel the void of not being represented, then they are unlikely to implement any change, and it continues. A simple example related to books within classrooms supports this. In 2020, it was found that only ten per cent of children's books had characters who were Black, Asian or members of other communities, and only seven per cent showed illustrations of characters from these backgrounds (Chetty et al., 2020). I know that this year was the first year I felt that I could dress up as a character that truly reflected me on World Book Day, so what does this feel like for children?

Following the outcry from the murder of George Floyd, there has been a huge increase in considering 'diversity and representation' within the Early Years. However, the idea of representation within the curriculum has been documented since 1990. The Rumbold Report (1990) states, 'Educators should also recognise and respond to the diversity of society, and the need to avoid stereotyping based on race, sex or special needs.' It goes on to explore how this is done and states, 'The aims will be to enable all children to respect and value ethnic and cultural diversity, to encourage positive self-images among ethnic minority children, and to ensure that high expectations attach to all groups alike.' Although the point of representation is made, there is no more thought as to how it may be implemented, what that may look like in the environment or why it may be important.

The Early Years Foundation Stage (2012) follows children's development from birth to the end of their Reception year. Current guidance places huge weight on play as a means for learning and exploration. Within the Early Years curriculum, there are seven different areas consisting of three prime areas (believed to be the foundations of learning) and four specific areas that are more focused. Each area is also broken up into subheadings of areas, for example, mathematics is split into 'number' and 'shape, space and measure'. The only references to culture or representation come under 'understanding the world – people and communities' (I am unsure why exploration of identity and self isn't in the more fitting area of 'PSHE – self-confidence and self-awareness'). Guidance given to practitioners about supporting this mentions having depictions of Black queens and pictures of children from around the world, sharing stories that reflect children's experiences, placing familiar items in role play areas, visiting churches and key areas in the community, and inviting visitors in.

I can honestly (and unfortunately) say that I have never seen this guidance implemented as consistent provision for children. Conversations about Diva lamps are made but are combined with 'Bonfire Night' as a generic celebration of 'lights'. Books are on shelves but only consist of stereotypical ideas of Africa. Lunar New Year is reduced to red rice in a sensory tray with no explanation.

The guidance is given as support for things that may help children meet these goals. Truly consider that the absolute minimum to ensure children have some opportunity to be celebrated and represented is simply some ideas to support provision and is not a given. During October, I saw social media conversations about how practitioners would not be focusing on Black History Month as they 'talk about differences all the time'. These same practitioners were quick to create Diva lamps three weeks later. It is ridiculous that children have to wait for their identities to be celebrated if and when practitioners see fit.

September 2021 sees new guidance comes into practice. This time there is more specific guidance to supporting children to have conversations about similarities between themselves and others. There is also now a subheading (still in 'understanding the world') focusing on 'noticing differences between people' for birth to three years or 'continue developing positive attitudes about the differences between people' for three- and four-year-olds (Department for Education, 2020b). This is done by providing books, play materials, and positive images with only one reference to race ('in consideration of Britain's diversity'). By the time these children reach Reception, this exploration is focused solely on religion and different celebrations.

The new guidance ensures that practitioners should be working on 'developing positive attitudes about the differences between people', which is a great start when considering how to celebrate and represent children. Is it enough by itself? Probably not. But it is the beginning at least.

Chantelle Douglas is a teacher with a number of years' experience in a range of primary schools, with a specialism within the Early Years. She has a strong interest and passion in introducing and embedding anti-racist practice within education.

Supporting children to develop a positive racial identity

I think back to my early childhood, and I find it hard to recall any toys that represented me. I remember having Barbie dolls, but my mum recalls that I used to cut their hair off. I often wonder what a therapist would say about this. Would they psychoanalyse me? Perhaps. On reflection, I wonder if this was a response to the fact that I didn't have hair like them. Was I angry in some way? Was I frustrated that I couldn't see myself? I wish I could ask my younger self. I do remember having one Black doll; however, it was not very culturally representative, and my mum said I often used it as a tool of fear to scare my younger brother. My mum believes it looked scary because it was a white doll with white features painted with black paint. It was lazy consumerism to get the Black pound.

Whilst my sons didn't have dolls, I did ensure that I sought as many culturally inclusive toys and books as possible. I took every opportunity in their earlier years to show them the value in their Black skin. I wanted to fill their bucket with as much joy as I could, so that they had enough in them to combat the racism that I knew they would inevitably endure later in life.

During the pandemic, I was reminded of how much I was going above and beyond to provide representation when I couldn't get the birthday card I wanted when my son turned ten. Usually, I would order a card with his picture on it. Problem solved. It was an easy way for him to always see himself. But due to the pandemic, the usual order service wasn't available. So, I thought the next best thing would be to buy a card with a child of colour from a supermarket. I went to all the major supermarkets. Not one child of colour on a birthday card. In 2020. Let that sink in. When did Black, Brown and other minoritised people arrive in the UK? 2021, it would seem…

We often do not see something as an issue when it doesn't affect us. But a clear example of White Privilege and structural advantage is knowing that books, cards, toys, magazines and newspapers will always represent those racialised as White. Yet for Black, Brown and other minoritised people, representation is rare, and if it is present, it will often be one voice, one view and stereotypically negative. After all, we are all the same, right?!

Representation is essential in helping children to develop a positive racial identity. If the supermarkets, the toy manufacturers and the media are failing to deliver on this, it becomes even more important for schools and nurseries to do this work. So, what do we need to be doing in schools and nursery settings to ensure high-quality representation and to support children in building a strong sense of self? Early Years expert Dr Stella Louis shares some advice to help us to work towards this goal.

Lived experience: Dr Stella Louis, Early Years consultant

The question of equality and diversity in the Early Years is not a new one. But now the Black Lives Matter movement has pushed the challenges faced by Black children in developing their racial identity to the fore. This contribution sets out to explore how children develop racial identity and self-image and why representation in the Early Years matters in shaping this.

The question we must start with is: how do children learn about their own racial identity? Right from birth, young children are learning to be themselves, figuring out what they like and want. All children (though they may be expected to conform to different cultural values by their families) are unique and have diverse experiences, needs and desires. If we are to challenge existing inequalities, we must acknowledge children's diverse experiences. An important aspect of a young child's development and learning is working out who they are, how they feel about themselves and where they fit into the world, family and setting. Race is inextricably linked with all aspects of learning about ourselves. This includes gender, language, disability, cultural practices, social class, habits and rituals.

Through their daily interactions with people, situations, objects and materials, all children receive powerful messages about themselves. These messages can have a negative or positive impact on their self-esteem and racial identity. If young children are frequently exposed to books containing images of people who do not look like them, or resources in the home corner which do not reflect their culture (such as cooking utensils, dressing-up clothes, hair and skin care, and multicultural food), then they will come to believe that their attributes are of little value – this will have a negative impact on their racial identity. All children need to see positive images of people who look like them to enable them to think that they too can be successful and this is especially important for children who are racially minoritised. Not seeing people like themselves represented in books and displays is one of the key barriers to developing a positive racial identity. This has a significant impact on young children being able to be themselves. I have heard so many heart-breaking stories from parents about their children either putting powder on their skin to become white or trying to rub their skin colour off in the bath or water tray. Sadly, even in 2021, these stories continue to be told. This highlights an urgent need to have resources in place which promote positive images of children and their families without them becoming tokenistic.

It is vital that children see meaningful images of people who look like them being represented in a positive way that celebrates and acknowledges difference. The lack of positive representations in Early Years schools and settings affects children's sense of belonging, racial identity and self-esteem. Young children are keen observers – they see how people with similar or different physical characteristics are represented and treated in the world around them. If children are frequently exposed to comments from other children such as, 'I don't want to be Black; I don't like them' or 'I don't want the Chinese doll', and educators are unable to support the child being excluded, then these comments reinforce racial prejudice. The more they are heard and felt, the more likely it is that the child will internalise such beliefs. This can be detrimental to their racial identity and self-image. Similarly, if children are exposed to discriminatory behaviours against themselves and others, these behaviours become learned and embedded in their thinking. This exposure then enables children to learn how to categorise or stereotype others or enact discriminatory behaviours, sometimes even positioning themselves as superior.

Children learn about themselves in their play and explorations – about who they are and what they might become as they try out different roles. They experiment with what they can do, without fear of failure, developing confidence and a sense of self-worth and identity. Children's attitudes towards difference and their disposition for learning are significantly affected by the feedback they receive from us. The way in which we respond to the behaviour of different children and our expectations of them can limit their ideas and beliefs about themselves. Do we respond more favourably in our expectations of children with whom we have an affinity than the children we do not? There is strong evidence to suggest that children's development and progression are influenced by our expectations of them. Unfair expectations and a lack of empathy with children is another key barrier. As a workforce we need to critically reflect on our individual capacity to work fairly and respectfully with all children and their families.

Developing practice

It is vital that we develop our practice in ways that ensure every child has meaningful opportunities to develop a positive racial identity. This process is a marathon rather than a sprint and it should be considered as ongoing. As a starting point, we need to review and debate the representations in our environments, carry out analysis of whether these representations celebrate diversity or reinforce stereotypes, and act upon our findings.

Let's now address two important interconnected issues. The first is the way in which we support children to have a positive self-image, so that they feel a sense of pride about their racial identity. The second is what we teach children about race.

Supporting each child to develop a positive self-image is a vital and important part of our work. It should not be underestimated. I believe that, in order to learn, young children need to feel comfortable in their own skin. An important part of our work with young children is helping them to understand how they are alike in some ways and how they can be different in others. We need to be able to encourage children to talk about their physical characteristics and those of others. This means supporting each child to recognise their individual qualities as well as the physical characteristics they share with others. This can be achieved by providing them with developmentally appropriate information about similarities and difference. We must offer support that enables children to develop understanding, respect, fairness and tolerance in their own way. Children notice differences in physical characteristics and may ask questions about their racial characteristics and those of other people. Here we must be role models for children, countering the learning of negative or stereotypical attitudes and behaviours towards difference when we see it enacted by others. We must deal with children's questions about race fairly, openly and honestly. It is important that we do not ignore their questions or attempt to change the topic to one we feel more comfortable in discussing. If talking about race makes us feel uncomfortable, we need to reflect on what gets in the way of addressing these issues with children. Open dialogue needs to occur within the wider setting about this issue, to raise awareness and engage all staff.

We create the social, emotional and physical learning environment. As a result, we must consider how we value cultural and physical diversity and how we learn about and respect it. This is an important consideration when thinking about what we want to teach children about race and racial identity. It is not just about the content of what we teach about race – it also includes how we counter negative attitudes and behaviours and how we develop positive adult–child relationships, so that children know and love who they are. Research suggests that if we create a learning environment where children can see themselves being reflected in representations of different customs, food, utensils and clothes, this can have a positive impact on children's levels of engagement.

Every child is unique and diverse and so, of course, is every Early Years setting. Settings need to come to an understanding about their own structural barriers that may help to maintain inequality of representation. There is cause for Early Years settings to actively promote diversity and inclusion, ensuring that all children and their families are represented. The responsibility to start conversations about similarities and differences that will lead to more positive representations – where children and families feel included, valued and represented – lies not just with owners and managers but all Early Years educators.

Dr Stella Louis is a freelance Early Years consultant. She originally trained as a NNEB nursery nurse and has 30 years' experience of working with children and families.

As educators, we are often fearful about conversations regarding race. We are worried that children are too young to have these conversations or are somehow convinced that talking to children about race and cultural difference will spoil them in some way. However, Black, Brown and racially minoritised children will experience the effects of racism from the moment they are born. If they are old enough to experience it, then White children are old enough to learn about it. The earlier we can teach children to celebrate cultural difference and understand racism is wrong, the better. Then perhaps we can have a generation of children who are able to genuinely tackle racism.

Our children need to be represented. We must start from abundance and celebrate them as much as we can. Joy is a wonderful experience. But this joy is stolen when all children do not get the opportunity to see themselves. We owe them that.

Summary

Key learning points

- Talk to your pupils about race. Take time to be curious and be honest with children when you do not know or understand. Use questions and statements such as, 'Help me to understand' or 'I don't know. Let us find out together.' This will allow you to explore together.
- Consider the appropriate strategies for talking to children about race at each child development phase.
- Review the resources and the literature you are using with children, including authors and protagonists, and consider what resources are available to children in your setting.
- If you are using any content or resources that might cause distress or trauma, for example, sources about slavery in a history lesson, think carefully about how they might affect the students in your class. Add a verbal and written trigger warning and give students the opportunity to express their emotions in a safe environment. Parents and carers should also be informed about the content that their children will receive.
- It is important that children do not only experience stories of Black and Brown people through the lens of pain and trauma. Educating about success and empowerment is important for all children, including those who are racialised as White.

Key question

As a child, how many toys, books and resources did you have that represented you?

a) I never considered it. I always had access to representation.
b) Most of my resources represented me.
c) I had a range of resources that equally represented a variety of cultural backgrounds.
d) I had few resources that represented me.
e) I didn't have any resources that represented me.

Further self-reflection questions

1. How early do you think we should talk to children about race?
2. Have you ever given safety instructions to a particular demographic of students? Why did you do this or why haven't you done this?
3. What resources do you think children should access to learn more about racial identity?
4. How would you facilitate conversations about race in your classroom?
5. At what point should White children be taught racial literacy?

Discussion points for staff meetings

- At a structural and institutional level, Black skin can be seen as threatening. Does this manifest itself in your behaviour policies?
- Have you ever allowed your fear of a child, based on societal attitudes, to affect the decisions you make and how you make them?
- If we do not talk to students about race, how do we prepare them for what we know exists in our society?

There are educators who believe children are too young to discuss race. The thinking is that children do not see colour and children can be protected from racism. This is not true. Every day Black, Asian and other minoritised children and young people experience racism. They witness it, they watch it in the media, they see it in their education. So, whose children are protected from racism if we don't discuss it at an early age?

4 What do the children think – and why is it so important that we hear them?

'Education is the most powerful weapon we can use to change the world.'
Nelson Mandela (1990)

I have worked in education for over ten years. I have had the privilege of working with so many wonderful children and have seen them develop and grow into amazing human beings. I always feel such a sense of gratitude. The experience of working with children is of mutual benefit: they keep me young; they keep my mind challenged; they force me to think about their future and the steps I am taking to create a future that they will want to live in.

Often, when people talk to me about the future, climate change is the first thing that comes to mind and in particular the powerful speech from Greta Thunberg at the 2019 United Nations Climate Action Summit in New York: 'Yet you all come to us young people for hope. How dare you? You have stolen my dreams and my childhood with your empty words, yet I am one of the lucky ones.'

As powerful as this is, I always cast my mind to Vanessa Nakate, a fellow climate change activist who was cut from a photograph of five young activists taken at a press conference in Davos. Vanessa had been the only Person of Colour in the picture. Initially, it was out of curiosity that she challenged the media outlet that had cropped the picture. She soon realised she had been a victim of anti-Black discrimination and racism. Vanessa received a wealth of support from various social activists, but for her this was a call to action. She said it was important for her to amplify voices, as 'climate activists of color are erased' (quoted in Evelyn, 2020). Vanessa spoke about other activists of colour who'd had similar experiences but felt afraid to speak their truth.

I spoke to several students about this. I wanted to know how the Black and Brown children in our school felt. The responses were clear, direct and to the point: 'Miss, we feel the same.' I wanted to know more, so I delved deeper into the discussion. Students then explained that they felt environmental activism was only for White people. One student said, 'Miss, imagine if I went to the Extinction

Rebellion march. Nobody would believe I was there because I care about the planet. They would think I was there to make trouble. Who do you think would get arrested first? It wouldn't be my White friends!'

I then spoke to a White student. I wanted to hear an alternative perspective. Did they see it in the same way? 'Oh yes, Miss. They couldn't come with us. I could shout in a police officer's face and as a young White girl I would be OK. My friend, although the same age, would be treated as a Black *man*. He would put himself at risk.'

The reality of this was not a surprise or a shock. But it triggered and unearthed racial trauma within me, trauma that I felt I had dealt with. I realised at this point that I had more unpacking to do.

In the summer of July 2020, I was supporting our 'Covid school' cohort, the group of students who were still attending school during the closures caused by the Covid-19 pandemic as their parents were key workers or needed additional support. It was after the Black Lives Matter march that had taken place over the weekend. One of my key students walked in. He had a t-shirt on that read BLACK LIVES MATTER. The atmosphere was thick and heavy. I could feel it wrapping itself around me. I was looking around the room, wondering if anyone would approach him in solidarity or challenge him for speaking out. He got closer to me and just looked into my eyes. I said to him, 'Are you OK?' He responded with a tiny whisper, 'Miss, you already know.' At that point the tears began to fill my eyes and the tears began to build in his. We looked at each other once more. It could not have been more than a second. But it felt like a lifetime of pain. Then we both turned around and walked away. Later that day, I went to find him. I asked why he chose to speak to me and he said, 'Miss, it's simple. I don't need to explain. You already know.'

Activity

Cast your mind back to the summer of 2020. George Floyd was murdered. It was a global media frenzy. There were still quite restrictive coronavirus measures in place, so you were likely still staying in your home. Black Lives Matter marches were taking place all over the world. Write a diary entry from that day from two perspectives:

1. a Black or Brown child
2. a White educator.

Consider these questions when writing your diary entry:

- What did you feel?
- What did you see, hear or experience?
- Who did you talk to?
- What steps did you take?

How to make sure your students are being heard

Listening to students and what they need is important. Children and young people should be at the centre of everything that we do. We should hear their lived experiences. As educators, we are often making decisions on behalf of our children, without seeing things through their lens. We need to consider all aspects of education and we need to facilitate opportunities for our students to voice their opinions on the educational experiences they are having in our setting. During my teaching career, I made it my mission to listen more than I spoke and to ask our young people to share their thoughts with me. They would often challenge me and ask why they couldn't see themselves in the curriculum. It was hard to answer. Why couldn't they? They should have been able to.

Listening to students also helps to develop our own racial literacy. For example, it is important for educators to understand the way in which language is utilised and interpreted within different cultures. A lack of understanding can lead to damaging consequences. My son had an experience where he used the word 'creaming' in class. Within our culture, we would say we 'cream' our skin rather than we 'moisturise' our skin, although it means the same thing. However, in this case, a teacher misinterpreted what he'd said and incorrectly told him off, as the word was interpreted to mean something sexual. I then had to discuss and explain this to my child. He also had the responsibility of educating his teacher on language and what it meant. Now the issue isn't just that the teacher didn't know or wasn't aware. That happens. The issue was the immediate jumping to a conclusion because of the teacher's lens of understanding and experience. Part of making sure students are being heard is refraining from making assumptions. Instead, be curious, ask questions, listen to the answers and acknowledge that there is always more than one perspective.

As we will see in Chapter 11, curriculum plays a crucial part in the process of developing racially literate students and creating a culture of anti-racist practice.

Yet I have heard many educators proudly boasting that racism does not happen in their school. Or that their own children do not see race or colour. But what does that assumption do to Black, Brown and racially minoritised children? What does it do to support the racial literacy of White children? Just because they do not speak out, it does not mean that they do not feel the impact. In addition to curriculum content, it's important to listen to the language children are using around race. They are often more equipped to have the conversation than adults. They are well informed and not afraid to learn.

In the following lived experience, we will consider representation in the curriculum from a student's perspective. Listen to what Shaheim has to say and then think about how you could invite your own students to share their views about representation in your school.

Lived experience: Shaheim Minzie, student

For our GCSE in English literature, we studied a set of 15 poems, all of which were to do with themes of identity and loss. In a class of predominantly Asian and Black students, we dissected Wilfred Owen's despair as young boys lost their innocence among the slew of bodies on battlefields. White poets had written these poems about issues that had never – and will never – affect us. While some Asian and Black men did fight in the First World War, these White poets write from a perspective that we do not share. My parents do not retell stories of my great-grandfather's past as he fought bravely for Britain because that story doesn't exist. Instead they tell me about the struggles of my grandmother, a Black, single mother raising 13 children in the 'ghetto' of Jamaica; how the opportunity to go beyond secondary education wasn't available for the majority. My dad, more often than I can count, reminds me that society will not pander towards me. The system has its squeaky, polished shoes on our necks. White war poets do not tell our stories of otherness and discrimination, conflict and confusion. They never will. In the midst of the growing consciousness surrounding racism in our society, an important question is how we can best benefit Black, Asian and racially minoritised students.

The government is responsible for deciding whether something *deserves* to be on the curriculum or not. They determine what is considered the 'essential knowledge' that students must know to be 'educated citizens', as stated in the aims of the National Curriculum in England (Department for Education, 2014a). In the 2019 General Election, only ten per cent of Members of the House of Commons were from ethnic minority backgrounds (Uberoi and Lees, 2020). Yes, it's appalling; you'd think that with minorities unprecedentedly entering spaces once denied to them, our political class would be a bit more diverse. The main thing to note is race vastly affects your experience.

Being Black (and minority ethnic), although it isn't unique to our experience, is growing up among the council houses of single mothers, stuck in a capitalist hamster wheel of work, home and sleep. Being Black is being three times more likely to be permanently excluded than White students. It isn't going to Eton, or any private school, and living in a White, upper-class, Conservative utopia. Our circumstances have prioritised what is vital to our upbringing and identity.

For my immigrant, Jamaican family, 'essential knowledge' would be learning about colonisation. It would be learning about the Civil Rights Movement, Jamaican history and Britain's infamously racist past. For me, it would be learning about Black diaspora, our activism and culture. Education should be comprehensive. It should include all accounts, from Sikhs fighting in war, the Notting Hill riots in 1958, and West Indians arriving on British land on the Empire Windrush. All the vibrantly loud stories of resistance and ethnic bravery should be on display, as much as the government displays of such exceptionalism in their glorification of Britain's questionable past.

So, we're almost done with the Power and Conflict cluster in our Year 10 English literature lesson. We're nine poems deep into linguistic analysis, our crumpled pages abused with pools of ink. My friends and I, being the only Afro-Caribbean students in the class, were particularly interested in this poem called *Checking Out Me History*, which was written in Jamaican Creole by John Agard. It's about the colonisation of education; it's about how education taught him about Dick Whittington but never taught him about Mary Seacole, about Lord Nelson but never Shaka. Does this sound familiar? Finally, we saw ourselves represented in a book of White poets. We saw our culture represented. Growing up, I didn't see much of myself, something that White children take for granted. There were no dolls or action figures with my Black skin, features, hair; White was and is the default. On children's TV, there were virtually no shows that had Black people as supporting characters, let alone main characters. To the extent that, in all our brittle, resistant, type 4 hair and dark skin, we believe that our narrative isn't deserving enough to be told. It lowers our self-esteem, making us feel 'alien' and 'different'. That belief is reiterated through our lives, repeated through the 84.7 per cent of White teachers in state-funded schools (Department for Education, 2021a), through the lack of Black and minority ethnic representation in the curriculum. Seeing yourself represented – your struggle, your experiences – creates a safe, inclusive space where, for once, you're being seen. Throughout *Checking Out Me History*, as John Agard's Creole permeated the English classroom, my dialect and culture were being shown. It was strangely vulnerable, having a part of me that I never saw in movies or read about in school libraries being heard. I felt seen.

However, it's equally as beneficial for Black and minority ethnic children as it is for White children. In Year 8 history, we learned about the American Civil Rights movement and significant points in America's fight for racial equality (Little Rock, Claudette Colvin, and so on); we learned about the transatlantic slave trade and colonisation. For White children too, 'essential knowledge' is learning about Black and minority ethnic history. It's the job of education to ensure that White children are socially conscious – that's done through studying modules like these in depth. It's the job of education to ensure that White children are equipped with the knowledge of how racism works and how it has been used as a tool to create division and their place as a White person in modern society. Ignorance breeds oppression. Whether it's something micro within their language or more macro and outwardly racist, White people get to litter 'mistakes' throughout their lives. They get to apologise for them and they are redeemed, absolved from any repercussions. In contrast, Black and minority ethnic people carry a built-up trauma for the rest of their lives because of said mistakes. Education and representation combat this.

*From his articles to youth work, **Shaheim Minzie** is a Bristolian student and writer, aspiring to be a part of the many carving an equal and fair future.*

Racial trauma

When the needs of Black, Brown and racially minoritised children are not heard and addressed, we see it manifest in several ways:

- lack of educational attainment
- overrepresentation in secure units and prison
- disproportionate exclusions (PRU to prison pipeline)
- over-policing
- health inequalities
- lack of representation in the curriculum
- racial trauma.

While these various manifestations are discussed at different points throughout this book, it is important to take a moment and reflect on racial trauma. Whilst

I am neither a therapist nor a psychologist, I have personally experienced and witnessed racial trauma. I still have therapy to address the experiences of my childhood and education that have scarred me.

Racial trauma occurs when a person is subject to ongoing racial abuse, racial bias, microaggressions and exposure to racial incidents. The discrimination that is experienced or witnessed is what causes the trauma and can be experienced directly or indirectly. Therefore, the act of repeatedly watching a summer of unarmed Black men being killed would have likely caused racial trauma to many of our students. This may have led to a summer of anxiety, depression, nightmares and confusion. Yet it's unlikely that this would have been addressed or that parents and carers would have been aware of where to get support. Many schools now use a trauma-informed approach to guide their pastoral practices and policies, but this approach fails to consider racial trauma. Racial trauma can be an adverse childhood experience (ACE; Bernard et al., 2021), and should be included alongside abuse, domestic violence or divorce in the list of ACEs teachers should be aware of. Racial trauma can also be transferred from generation to generation, meaning that it is something that a considerable number of Black, Brown and racially minoritised children will experience. Trauma affects our children physically and mentally and impacts upon their nervous system. It is important that we take time to understand racial trauma and think about the role that we play as educators to support children who are exposed to it. It is not enough to leave it to Child and Adolescent Mental Health Services (CAMHS) or our school counsellors. It is something we must challenge and support through our school culture and values. To learn more about racial trauma, read Resmaa Menakem's (2021) book *My Grandmother's Hands*.

Causes

The anxiety and stress that trigger racial trauma can take a number of forms:

- **Direct racial abuse or discrimination:** This may be a physical attack, verbal abuse, racist slurs and stereotyping.
- **Racial gaslighting:** This may occur when others do not take racism seriously, questioning if the experience was real or asking a student or colleague to explain.
- **Racial abuse of family members or loved ones:** This may be overt or covert racism. It could be unwanted attention or jokes. This is particularly difficult when Black, Brown and racially minoritised people are a minority in an environment and are expected to code-switch to fit into an environment that is unsafe.

- **Witnessing members of a marginalised group receive racist abuse:** This can happen via social media or could be witnessed first-hand.
- **Racial stereotyping:** This may occur when students are continually told that they perform better or worse than others at particular tasks.
- **Fear:** This could occur when a student may be afraid to share what they are experiencing as they are worried that they will not be listened to and will receive the blame.
- **Being refused medical treatment:** The assumption may be that the student has been the perpetrator rather than the victim.

I remember sitting watching the news with my ten-year-old son. Watching image after image of Black protestors being hurt, the reoccurring image of George Floyd being murdered, and shots being fired into neighbourhoods. I still replay that conversation in my head. 'Mummy, why do they hate us so much?' 'Son...' my voice cracked, tears rolled down my face and I turned away. Because in that moment, he didn't feel safe. I didn't feel safe.

Impact

Racial trauma can impact:

- **Relationships:** This includes teacher-to-student relationships.
- **School work:** Racial trauma can lead to a lack of interest or an inability to complete tasks.
- **Safety:** Students can feel fear and a lack of safety.
- **Child development:** Racial trauma can have an impact on a student's physical and emotional health.

These experiences may become isolating. Students may feel humiliated and they might sense a loss of connection with the wider world and an ultimate fear for their life.

Symptoms and support

Often the symptoms of racial trauma may be ignored or misdiagnosed. Racial trauma has an impact on health and wellbeing and in extreme cases can cause post-traumatic stress disorder. There needs to be an understanding that the responses to racial trauma can take many forms and it may not manifest itself in one way or form. Symptoms could include:

- intense anxiety and fear
- recurring negative thoughts
- hyper-sensitivity
- avoidance
- anger and aggression.

It is important that educational settings do not shy away from this and understand that racial trauma may play out differently in different phases of child development. Environment and culture can impact how it is perceived. One person may be extremely angry, whereas another may become intensely scared and refuse to attend school. Responses must not be blanket. Black, Brown and racially minoritised children must not be treated as a homogeneous group.

Schools have the opportunity to support children and young people with racial trauma and to create space for healing to take place.

- Give children time to heal.
- Equip all staff with a basic understanding of racial trauma.
- Have named staff who are trained with trauma-informed approaches that are racism-specific.
- Support children to talk to those they trust.
- Give children opportunities to talk about race and access to other children who may have shared lived experiences.
- Build links with the school's local community.
- Ensure that children have access to culturally sensitive healing and therapeutic support from a professional.
- Provide supervision for pastoral support staff.
- Build a culture of openness.
- Understand that racial trauma may also impact staff from Black, Brown and racially minoritised communities.

Summary

Key learning points

- Listening to the lived experiences of your students is essential. We must give our students the opportunity to speak out and to tell us what they need, and crucially we must then act on what we hear. If students' needs are not addressed, this can lead to racial trauma.
- Racial trauma is deep rooted. It can occur directly and indirectly. It is important to ensure the correct support systems are in place. Staff must be adequately trained and be aware of places to signpost parents and carers for support. It is not enough to acknowledge it; we must do something about it.

Key question

How often do you stop and listen to the experiences of the children in your class?

a) That is for tutor time.

b) They talk during their PSHE lessons.

c) Only when they have an issue or concern.

d) It is an intentional practice woven into my everyday educational toolkit.

Further self-reflection questions

1. Why are we denying Black, Asian and racially minoritised students an opportunity to understand their roots?
2. What would happen if educators ensured that active listening took place in their settings?
3. In what ways can these conversations be facilitated?

Discussion points for staff meetings

- How is the current trauma-informed approach that is being widely cited in schools addressing racial trauma? Or is this another example of racial exclusion?

5 What language do we use when we talk about race?

'To educate as a practice of freedom is a way of teaching that anyone can learn.'
bell hooks (1994)

Why are conversations regarding race so fundamental in education in the twenty-first century?

To treat conversations regarding race as a thing of the past is not only problematic, but also an erasure of the trauma experienced by many people's ancestors and the trauma that continues to manifest itself today.

Some educators will argue that continuing to bring conversations regarding race and racism to the table creates further division. So, should we let it go? After all, it is in the past. Or is it? Other educators will argue that given the continued trauma and racism that Black, Brown and racially minoritised people experience, we need to educate ourselves, reflect on ourselves and on our action. We must be accountable and empower the next generation with what they need to be better than the generations before them.

It is argued that discussions on race and racism can be political and that schools are not a place for partisan views. But as an educator, I believe that these conversations are imperative. To ensure that all children and young people are safe in school, we need to be aware of how we talk about race and racism and the language we use. Often racism is talked about as a behaviour issue, but it runs so much deeper than that.

The fact is that discussions about race are not the issue *per se*. The issue is the racism that follows, when bias, discrimination and structural advantage take over, because discussions about race have been dealt with and taught poorly and the same cycles are perpetuated. When overt and covert racism seeps in and impacts the lives of Black people and People of Colour. Some conversations lead us to comparing our own country with others and we find comfort when we say, 'Well, it is worse over there', or at least, 'We are not as bad as other countries', but as Dave stated in his performance at the BRIT Awards in 2020, being the least racist is still racist.

Therefore, we have to find the language to have these discussions in the best way possible.

My mum recently attended a barbecue and was the only Black woman there. A young girl about four years old approached her and stared in amazement. She then said to my mum, 'Are you wearing make-up?' My mum responded by saying yes. The little girl then said, 'But why brown?' My mum then realised that the girl was referring to her skin. It was her first interaction and experience of meeting a Black person. When I heard this story, what I was very aware of was that the language used and what followed next would impact this little girl and her understanding of race.

For education to play its part, for things to change, race has to be tackled in schools. We are tasked with educating generation after generation to become global citizens. But how do we do that when we do not have the language necessary to start the conversation? Too often fear is preventing us from challenging, discussing, calling out and calling in. This reluctance to talk about race and racism stems from a lack of knowledge, or in many instances the current knowledge that has been taught. This can create an arrogance and confidence that these issues no longer need to be talked about. However, the reality is that we have been taught our history through a particular lens and from a particular point of view, but with the erasure of the voices of those who have had the relevant lived experience.

Question

How confident do you feel about leading conversations about race in the classroom? Do you have the language necessary to facilitate these discussions?

Lived experience: Donna Whitcliffe, educator

To understand the British education system, you must look back to its historical roots. A degree in sociology and social policy provided me with the opportunity to interrogate and delve into the British education system. When you look at the origins of the British education system, initially education was only afforded to wealthy (landed) men and only they could vote. As the masses pushed for voting and other social and economic rights, coupled with the mechanisation of farming, education was a way to control the general population. Concede a little so that they won't ask for more!

State education was about educating for an available labour force. The landed gentry maintained their power through private education, which still largely continues today. The British education system was designed to keep the masses quiet, ensuring they weren't making too many demands or challenging the power structure. It was not created with Black, Asian and racially minoritised children in mind.

The 1950s and 1960s saw many people arriving from the Caribbean and other British colonies into the UK. It is interesting to wonder that whilst people of the colonies were actively encouraged by the British government to help rebuild post-war Britain, how and why did many Britons believe these people came to 'take their jobs'? A similar cry has been made more recently with people from eastern European countries entering the UK. Where and how did this propaganda show itself? The majority, if not all, of the Caribbean countries had and still do have education systems based on the British system. Examination papers are sent from the Caribbean to the UK to be marked and graded. However, many found that whilst they may have been educated, their qualifications gained in the Caribbean did not translate to the British equivalents, even though to all intents and purposes they were the same qualifications. This led to many having to take jobs far below their skill set and supply their labour in the main to factories, the National Health Service and transport systems at the unskilled end of the workforce. Being employed as unskilled labour also intersected with and was compounded by unequal pay.

So, a generation who came for economic gain found themselves on the back foot, facing vast amounts of racism in all areas of their daily activities. Be it education, employment, housing, healthcare or economics, racism and inequality were faced at every turn. Even though, as citizens of the colonies, they were invited to the UK, there had been no thought as to their social needs. It was as though they were expected to go home at weekends and have no need for housing, education, healthcare and so on, as no provision had been made for this.

In schools, there were low expectations of children from Caribbean communities and many of these children were labelled as 'special needs' due to racism and ignorance in equal measures. An example of this is given by Akala (2018) as he writes in *Natives* about how he found himself in one of these 'special needs' groups. We are still fighting against such injustices today; we still, some 50 years later, are battling curriculum content and delivery. At best, half-truths are still being peddled to White British children and, at worst, downright lies.

In 1999, Professor Stephen May published a book entitled *Critical Multiculturalism* and in it he cited a government department that said, 'Individual people in these islands have much in common, but they also have individual characteristics specific to a country, ethnic grouping, religions, gender and social class. We do not believe that school history can be so finely tuned to accommodate all of these details all of the time. Still, at least it can make pupils aware of the richness and variety of British culture and its historical origins.' (Department for Education and Skills, cited in May, 1999). Whilst May was writing in 1999, his questions are still alive today: 'How is everyday racism produced and reproduced within the educational system? The school simultaneously holds out the promise of mobility and opportunity, yet at the same time teaches and reinforces hierarchy and stratification in its day-to-day operations. What are the social processes in everyday practices through which ideologies of superiority and inferiority are reproduced? Three areas stand out: firstly, the content of education, secondly, hierarchies of language and thirdly the hidden curriculum.' (May, 1999)

We need an honest curriculum, particularly in respect of history. The curriculum cannot just cover slavery, which implies there was nothing before. History should be told from 360 degrees and not from a blinkered Eurocentric worldview. Yes, Britain was great – but how did it become 'great'? Who and what suffered loss in order for Britain to be 'great'? If British history is taught honestly from this 360-degree perspective, all histories would be included. Discuss the British Museum contents and the knowledge, skills and cultures that produced such items, as opposed to just talking about the great institutions.

Whilst at university I experienced racism, which left me wondering how much my race would potentially impact my final grade, having written an assignment about how the Aboriginal people had been pushed off their land and had their children removed as they were deemed poor parents. I received a low grade for this assignment. I wrote another assignment using all Black authors. My lecturer said that he did not recognise any of the authors even though each one had been referenced correctly in the bibliography. The only book in the library at the time with any reference to Blackness was written by an old White man who rubbished the idea of Afrocentricity and culture. This experience resulted in a change of direction in my education. The whole experience led me to thinking that if an adult had such struggles at university, what were children to expect at primary and secondary level?

The media and other institutions have a large part to play in how whole groups of people are regarded in general, but education is a starting point. The school curriculum needs an overhaul. In being truthful about British history and including the history and achievements of others, all children benefit. We are at a tipping point: do we make that change or do we perpetuate the lies to future generations?

Donna Whitcliffe has worked for more than 25 years with families, young people and the local community in education, community activism and adult education within a variety of settings.

But how do I talk about race?

One of the most common questions I am asked is 'But how do I talk about race? What language should I use?', or I hear statements such as 'But I don't want to get it wrong. Can you give a list of things I can say?' The reality is we just need to start.

However, before we start, we do need to be sure that we are literate and prepared for the challenges that lie ahead. Take the time to gain knowledge, understand the context and be prepared to be uncomfortable and challenged. Give space to be heard and do not assume. Curiosity is vital. The following four agreements (based on Ruiz, 2018) will help to frame in a simplistic way the commitments you need to make when having these conversations:

1. Be impeccable with your work.
2. Do not take it personally. It is so easy to have a victim mentality and let guilt and defensiveness take over.
3. Do not assume. Allow your mind to be curious and open and do not let stereotypes limit you.
4. Do your best. This changes at times.

I would also add stamina to this list. It is important not to let fatigue stop you from your commitment. There are times when you are exhausted. But if you aren't racialised yourself, remember for those for whom it is their lived experience, it never stops.

Lived experience: Bob Hawxwell, drama and performing arts teacher

As a White privileged male, I find myself thinking that there are two positions one can find oneself in on the subject of race: either blissfully ignorant or perpetually guilty. The former position is the one that either genuinely or consciously refuses to see race and thereby avoids any of the awkward issues connected with the subject. The second is an acknowledgement that you could and should be doing more. I think it is fair to say that on reflection I have been in both camps during my career as an educator.

Margaret Thatcher famously summarised her view of an education system that was ideologically rather than educationally driven by claiming that learners were being taught 'anti-racist maths' in many schools. The example of mathematics, whether true or not (a debatable point), was carefully chosen to emphasise the lengths 'the liberal left' would go to indoctrinate young people because, after all, what has racism got to do with learning mathematics?

Thatcher's allegation formed part of a broader argument that placed education firmly in an economic context (knowledge and qualifications leading to employment) rather than a social one (Thatcher famously declared there was no such thing as society). This view of the education system enabled those working within it to make themselves entirely comfortable with the idea that learning their subject was not an issue of race and that their classroom was made up of learners pure and simple, and not learners from a range of ethnic, cultural and economic backgrounds (in other words, the 'I don't see colour' mantra).

For those of us teaching humanities subjects, the issue of race was less easy to brush under the carpet. For myself, trained as a drama teacher but employed initially as a teacher of GCSE English, I think I could have waltzed quite happily into my teaching career (in a suburban all-White comprehensive) without any consideration of race or representation. I had had virtually no training on the subject of race and representation on my very White PGCE course. The only Black student on the course gave a presentation on the topic. Still, all it did was reinforce our smug, self-congratulatory sense of being not racist, rather than making us consider any issues of how race could and should be addressed in the classroom.

In 1988, many schools operated a policy of all learners taking English and English literature GCSEs simultaneously and the choice of books for study was left entirely to the individual school. This was the start of my teaching career and I took over a Year 11 class whose next set book for English literature was *Roll of Thunder, Hear My Cry* by Mildred D. Taylor. The heroine of the story, set in 1930s Mississippi, is Cassie Logan, a young Black girl who through a number of set pieces throughout the book learns about racism in general and 'Jim Crow' in particular. My secondary position on race matters almost immediately kicked when confronted by the text: the reason? I had one Black student in my class. An all-White class would have been a far easier prospect. I could encourage all of them to reflect on the appalling instances of racial discrimination detailed in the book: Cassie being given a school book that had been passed down through so many 'Whites-only' schools that it was falling to bits and was therefore stamped as being 'suitable for n*****', or Cassie being severely reprimanded for not stepping off the kerb into the muddy street to allow a little White girl to pass.

But with a Black girl in my class, how could I ignore the fact that being Black was not just about characters in a book? It was about her and her life, and I was frankly scared of how she might feel reading this book. What was worse was that I had no idea how to deal with the situation, or even if there was a situation. What I did was to talk to the student on her own and ask her how she felt about the subject matter of this book. She appeared surprised that I was asking her. In her view it was a book she needed to study for her qualification. She was an able, diligent learner, and that was that. I don't recall at the time feeling anything other than relief at her response. I criticised myself: had this girl experienced racism of any kind? I didn't ask her. Did she feel treated the same as other learners? I didn't ask her. As a class, we all slipped into the cosy White liberal mindset that clearly identified that whilst racism was bad, it was something that happened to other people, in a different place and a different time. It was not about us.

Bob Hawxwell has been a drama and performing arts teacher since 1988 and is now retired. He was the director of performing arts at Cox Green Specialist School from 2005 to 2012.

The importance of understanding and talking about Whiteness

Language is power: but who has the power? Those who hold the power own the language. This is why it's only recently that terms like White Privilege have become common. 'White Privilege' is confronting and difficult to digest and can often result in anger and defensiveness. It's no surprise that it hasn't become part of our language until recently – when that language has been owned by White people. Peggy McIntosh (1989) talks about the invisible knapsack as an analogy for White Privilege: White people have unearned assets and experiences that they cash in on a daily basis. White Privilege does not mean that White people do not experience hardship or difficulty; instead, it refers to the fact that any hardship experienced will not be due to their race.

Activity

Think about the following questions. This could be an individual reflection activity or a group discussion or mind map activity.

- Write down three examples of unearned advantage that you have experienced in your life.
- Write down three examples of unearned disadvantage that you have experienced in your life.

Talking about Whiteness is a central part of unpicking our understanding of race and racism and I'd like to hand over to Dr Matt Jacobs (PhD) to explore this more deeply. Matt is a researcher, educator and speaker whose PhD thesis discusses how White, middle-class men are responding to Black Lives Matter and #MeToo to defend the privilege that their intersecting Whiteness, masculinity and middle-classness affords them. Matt uses this research to inform his piece below.

Whiteness and White Privilege, by Dr Matt Jacobs (PhD), Director of Wide Open Voices Ltd

Whiteness is not just about being racialised as White or having 'white' skin. It is not simply about appearance. Whiteness is also about how White people make sense of society and how they understand it to work. Critically, Whiteness is a perspective, or 'standpoint' (Frankenberg, 1993), through which White people see themselves and the Black and Brown communities of the Global South. Whiteness is a racialised perspective that conditions White people's behaviour, decisions, actions, beliefs, and attitudes – conscious or unconscious, and as such, it is a social phenomenon that has a tangible impact on the world.

The dominant values, beliefs and ideologies of the standpoint of Whiteness of today have been in the making for centuries. We could go back to the Eurocentric re-racialising of Jesus into a white-skinned, blue-eyed, blonde-haired man by Western interpretations of Christianity. This is an aspect of the narratives by White European men and churches that claim God made 'man' in his image, i.e. anyone who was not White was not human. These narratives were used to justify innumerable horrors perpetrated against Indigenous peoples as White Europeans 'discovered' the world.

We could go back to the philosophers of the 1700s such as Hume, Voltaire and Kant, all of whom proclaimed the superiority of White men over all others. By way of an example, in 1742 David Hume said, 'I am apt to suspect the Negroes... to be naturally inferior to the Whites. There never was any civilized nation of any other complexion than White.' We could go back to the Enlightenment era scientists who re-expressed these narratives under the guise of scientific reasoning. These arguments were used to justify the enslavement of the indigenous people of the continent of Africa as the narratives constructed them as not just inferior to White people but also less than human. We could look at the statements made by politicians throughout the 1800s and 1900s that repeated these same narratives to justify imperialism, colonial segregation, and assert the right of White men to rule all others. We could look at how these narratives have been repeated throughout the years to today – for example in how those such as Enoch Powell, Margaret Thatcher, Nigel Farage (Asthana and Mason, 2016), Katie Hopkins (Williams, 2015), Nick Ferrari (Lothian-McLean, 2020), and the *Sun* and the *Daily Mail* in general have spoken about People of Colour, particularly in relation to immigration to Britain.

We could examine advertising and popular entertainment over the years to see how these narratives of White superiority are repeated through these mediums as well. From the soap adverts in the 1800s that depicted images of happy, smiling Black children after being 'washed' White to more contemporary skincare products offering free apps to South Asian men that would lighten their skin colour on their Facebook profile pictures; from the repeated hyper-sexualisation and objectification of Black women and representation of Black men as 'gangstas' and 'thugs' in popular music and the repeated trope of the Muslim terrorist in TV dramas to the narrative of the helpless and uncivilised Black people in need of being saved by White people in fundraising campaigns by international charities. The narratives are repeated.

The crucial point to understand here is that the repeated historic and present-day narratives of White superiority and of criminality, barbarity and threat about People of Colour are the narratives of ideological White supremacy. These narratives of White supremacy have told White audiences things that they have come to believe to be truths about the world. These are supposed 'truths' that White people have, usually uncritically and ultimately unconsciously, subscribed to; 'truths' that condition the way White people see themselves and People of Colour; 'truths' that inform the standpoint of Whiteness. The way the standpoint of Whiteness conditions how White people see and talk about People of Colour in inferior terms is also sometimes referred to as the 'White gaze', as it is a way of looking that constructs the world according to the precepts of Whiteness and White supremacy.

This standpoint of Whiteness continually informs how White people think and behave in relation to others. In essence, it conditions their everyday actions. In her 2003 book *Race and Social Analysis,* Knowles refers to these everyday actions as a process of 'race-making'. In this process the standpoint of Whiteness defines racial others in discriminatory ways and conditions how White people engage with Black, Asian and minoritised people on a day-to-day basis. These everyday social processes can, then, be understood as the set of cultural practices through which Whiteness is performed and it is through this 'myriad of everyday social processes' (Knowles, 2003) that White people produce and reproduce racial inequality.

However, because the cultural practices of Whiteness are performed through everyday processes, they are seen by White people as normal and are, as Frankenberg points out, unmarked and unremarked upon. In fact, the narratives that have conditioned the standpoint of Whiteness to be discriminatory to People of Colour have also constructed being White and the cultural practices of Whiteness as the normal and acceptable cultural practices of society. They are, in essence, invisible to White people, although they have been painfully visible to Black and Brown communities of the Global South for centuries.

This invisible and unmarked aspect of the cultural practices of Whiteness is why you don't hear White people talking about White culture, White history, White music, White arts, White food and White literature but you will hear them refer to Black literature, Black music, Black arts, ethnic clothes, ethnic food, ethnic dance, and so on. This is one example of how Whiteness is obscured and made normal, and the cultural practices of Black and Brown communities of the Global South are named, marked and, in their differences from these 'normal' White cultural practices, judged as 'exotic', 'backwards' and 'inferior' in some way.

In contrast, the normalised cultural practices of Whiteness, particularly those of middle-class Whiteness, are presented as respectable and acceptable. Those people recognised as White and performing these practices appropriately are favoured by society. It is these cultural practices of Whiteness that create White Privilege by perpetuating a society that is set up to benefit White people. However, just as these cultural practices that judge and discriminate against 'others' are held to be normal by White people, the privileges that arise from these discriminations are also understood to be normal. This is why so many White people struggle with acknowledging and accepting that they have White Privilege. When being privileged is normal, it isn't seen or understood as a privilege. It's just normal, right?

But what exactly is White Privilege?

Amidst the current political attacks on White Privilege in the UK, it is important that we have an accurate and informed understanding of what White Privilege really is. Whether the attacks be from Minister for Levelling Up Communities and Minister for Equalities Kemi Badenoch stating that teaching about White Privilege is unlawful (quoted in Murray, 2020), Education Secretary Nadhim Zahawi stating that it is a 'contested view' and constitutes 'partisan politics' (quoted in Harding, 2021), or the Commons Education Committee (2021) saying teaching White

Privilege could be against the Equality Act, they all promote a misrepresentation of the concept of White Privilege. This is a politicised misrepresentation that seeks to conflate race privilege and class privilege in a process that weaponises class against Black, Asian and minoritised people. It also works to deny the reality that the disadvantage White, working-class people experience is down to middle-class privilege and is nothing to do with race.

Despite what the Education Committee Report claims, teaching White Privilege is *not* about telling children, or adults, that they are different because of their race. It is about educating people that our society is iniquitous and is set up to favour people who are racialised as White. Teaching children about the dynamics and causes of White Privilege is teaching them about social justice, which must be a fundamental pillar of the education system, if we are ever to achieve an equitable and truly inclusive society.

White Privilege itself exists in a number of forms, for example, material, structural, emotional and psychological, but critical to the understanding of privilege is that the benefits of it are 'unearned' and have nothing to do with how hard someone has worked or how much wealth they have. Those who have White Privilege have done nothing in order to gain it. Society affords it to them simply because society is set up to favour White people. From a systemic perspective, the everyday cultural practices of Whiteness inform not just day-to-day interactions but also how White people in positions of power make decisions, develop policies and procedures, write legislation, determine right and wrong, and so on. Combined with day-to-day practices, these create a system of power that results in a society that is set up to benefit White people; a society in which White people accrue benefits simply because of the colour of their skin; a society in which all Black, Asian and minoritised people are discriminated against. In summary, then, Whiteness is the racialised perspective that conditions White people's cultural practices, which create the systems of power that result in structural, institutional and cultural racism and the pervasiveness of ideological White supremacy and White Privilege.

Racism and being anti-racist

We need to be clear that racism is more than just holding prejudicial beliefs about a person because of the colour of their skin. In truth, racism is a combination of holding racially prejudicial beliefs whilst also wielding power, and this is not simply about the individual power that a teacher or principal might hold, but about a system of power. The positions of power White people have held now, and throughout our history, have allowed us to convert the prejudiced attitudes towards Black and Brown communities of the Global South into legislative policies, organisational practices and cultural norms (Pease, 2010). This has created and maintains today a racist system of power through which all Black, Asian and minoritised people are discriminated against. To put this into stark context, all Black, Asian and minoritised people in Britain will experience racism because of this system of power, even if they never meet a White person.

The implications of this should be clear to us all. In Britain and other White-majority countries, only White people can be racist because only White people have control over systems of power in this country. Black, Asian and minoritised people do not have control over any systems of power that could result in all White people being discriminated against. Whilst a Person of Colour can make negative statements about White people that reference the colour of their skin, this is not racism as it is not accompanied by a racist system of power. It exists simply as an 'incident' of racialised prejudice and has no real impact on White people other than, perhaps, to trigger White fragility in those who hear or read it.

The fact that only White people have access to, control over, and benefit from this racist system of power has further implications. It means that White people cannot be non-racist. White people are either anti-racist or racist. Not actively challenging racism makes us complicit in it – silence *is* violence. Furthermore, for a White person to say they aren't racist whilst continuing to uncritically enjoy the privileges being White affords them and not actively do anything about racism actually reinforces and further embeds it into the society. As such, all White people, just like I do, have an obligation and responsibility to be actively anti-racist. To be anti-racist, we must act, we must disrupt Whiteness. So, what can we do? How can we disrupt Whiteness and so disrupt racism?

As a White, middle-class man, I do not presume to have the right or the requisite knowledge to tell Black, Asian and minoritised people what to do to disrupt Whiteness. I do not have the lived experience and cannot comprehend what that experience is like. My responsibility and my place as a White person is, I believe, to talk to other White people about what we can do. This is not intended to be exclusionary, and I apologise if it feels that way for any Black, Asian and minoritised people reading this book. It is intended to be a call to White people to address our Whiteness as part of the overall work to eradicate racism from society. So, what can we do?

Take responsibility

The first and most important step is to take responsibility. Take responsibility for the historic and current racism that exists in society. If you feel guilt or shame, keep it to yourself and assuage it by taking responsibility and taking action. Expressions of guilt or shame often only serve to re-centre Whiteness and White people in the conversation, which further marginalises the voices of those who are oppressed by the racism we are feeling guilt and shame over. This is often referred to as 'White guilt' or 'White tears' to emphasise its performative nature. So, keep your feelings out of the conversations. Instead, take responsibility and take action.

Challenge your perspective
Educate yourselves. Take a look at the lists on page 93. Read the books on the reading list; watch movies and TV shows on the watching list that show Black, Asian and minoritised people in lead roles and in their full humanity; listen to the podcasts on the listening list; and listen to Black, Asian and minoritised colleagues but critically do not ask them to educate you. Do not ask them to undertake the emotional labour for you. It is not their job. Do not ask them to talk with you but, when they talk, give them space to do so and just listen.

Be intentionally conscious
In this process of educating yourself, think deeply, openly and honestly about the ways in which you see the world and the ways in which you perform Whiteness. Then change them. Constantly reflect on whether what you are thinking and doing is driven by Whiteness, and question whether what you think is normal is, in fact, oppressive. Train yourself to see the messages of Whiteness that exist in what you see and hear on a day-to-day basis and question them both with yourself and with the people around you.

Learn critical questioning
Racism is not founded on any solid rationale. Justifications and explanations of racism are always based on a flawed logic. When you witness racism or hear people expressing racist opinions, ask critical questions about what they are saying or doing. These can be as simple as 'Why do you think that?', 'What do you think is the reason…?' and 'How would it be if…?'. This approach forces people to interrogate their own perspectives, can expose the flawed logic of them, and provides an opportunity for you to talk with them about other ways of seeing and understanding the world.

It must be stated that, as a White person with no generational or personal lived experience of racism directed at myself, I do not and cannot have the same affective response to hearing racism as Black, Asian and minoritised people. Indeed, where I hear racism, a Black, Asian or minoritised person is experiencing that racism. As such, my engagement with it will be less visceral and certainly not triggering. So, what I advocate here may be easier and safer for a White person to do and is an example of how White people can use their White Privilege to challenge racism.

Be active as a White anti-racist

Go out of your way to make conscious, anti-racist decisions in your day-to-day life. Seek out Black-, Asian-, and minority-ethnic-owned shops and businesses. Buy the books on the reading list from Black-owned bookstores or publishers. If you don't know of any, use the links on page 93 to find one. Talk to your school's procurement function and determine if they operate a policy that proactively seeks to buy from Black-, Asian-, and minority-ethnic-owned businesses; if they don't, lobby them to develop one.

Be visible as a White anti-racist

Challenge any racism and the operations of Whiteness you witness, even in yourself and be open about it. Highlight what you see and understand to other White people. Use the knowledge you gain from your learning and critical questioning skills to challenge and to change the narrative.

Call out Whiteness and make it visible

White people making Whiteness visible challenges it at its core. Call out its normativity, point out to others how what appears to be 'normal' is in fact oppressive.

Here's a simple exercise you can do to make Whiteness visible. For the next week, in work, at home, when you are out for an evening, wherever you are, when you refer to a White person, actually use the word 'White' in that reference. For example, 'Can you ask the White barman for another bag of crisps, please?' Or 'Did you see what that White man was wearing?' This will have the effect of upsetting the normal and invisible aspect of Whiteness. It may also instigate conversations with others because they may ask you why you are doing it. That will give you the opportunity to use your learning and awareness to have conversations about Whiteness and racism with your colleagues and your friends.

Be mindful of the pitfalls of allyship

Whilst White people have a responsibility to be actively anti-racist, we have to remain conscious of our role in the work. Be careful that your White Privilege does not result in you taking up space that Black, Asian and minoritised people should be leading in. Be aware that the perspective of Whiteness and the legacy of the colonial 'civilising mission' can lead to patronising benevolence in which our allyship becomes a mechanism through which Black, Asian and minoritised people are minimised and further oppressed. Make sure that your 'allyship' is not performative; that it is not simply a performance to assuage any guilt you feel or to deflect criticism of Whiteness away from you; that it is not a performance that does not actually disrupt racism but in effect reinforces Whiteness. Equally, do not refer to yourself as an 'ally', as this can articulate White saviourism in which we construct Black, Asian and minoritised people as lacking the agency for self-liberation and needing us to save them. They don't.

Finally, if you are White, there is a key factor to be aware of in all that you do. It is only by taking responsibility for Whiteness, in its structural, systemic and cultural forms, in our embodiment of it and our performance of it in our everyday practices, that we can disrupt it. Remember, White people are either racist or anti-racist. Choose which you are going to be.

Reading list

So, You Want to Talk about Race by Ijeoma Oluo

Why I'm No Longer Talking to White People About Race by Reni Eddo-Lodge

White Fragility: Why it's so hard to talk to White people about race by Robin DiAngelo

White Privilege: The myth of a post-racial society by Kalwant Bhopal

Me and White Supremacy: How to recognise your privilege, combat racism and change the world by Layla Saad

Brit(ish): On race, identity and belonging by Afua Hirsch

Natives: Race and class in the ruins of empire by Akala

The Good Immigrant by Nikesh Shukla

Between the World and Me by Ta-Nehisi Coates

How to Be an Antiracist by Ibram X. Kendi

The Power of Privilege: How White people can challenge racism by June Sarpong

Hood Feminism: Notes from the women White feminists forgot by Mikki Kendall

I'm Still Here: Black dignity in a world made for Whiteness by Austin Channing Brown

Uncomfortable Conversations with a Black Man by Emmanuel Acho

Black Fatigue: How racism erodes the mind, body, and spirit by Mary-Frances Winters

Empireland: How imperialism has shaped modern Britain by Sathnam Sanghera

Black and British by David Olusoga

Lists of Black-owned bookshops

www.stylist.co.uk/books/uk-bookshops-diverse-black-authors-books-online/396930

https://ukblackwritersforum.wordpress.com/black-book-shopspublishers

Listening list (podcasts)
We Need to Talk about Whiteness, The Podcast
About Race with Reni Eddo-Lodge
No Country for Young Women, Sadia Azmat and Monty Onanuga
The Echo Chamber Pod
Slay in Your Lane, Yomi Adegoke and Elizabeth Uviebinené
The Good Ancestor, Layla F. Saad
Pod Save the People, DeRay Mckesson

Watching list (films and television shows)
Queen Sugar; Insecure; Dear White People; The Carmichael Show; Black-ish; Grown-ish; Atlanta; 2 Dope Queens; Black Panther; A Wrinkle in Time; Get Out; Girls Trip; Sorry to Bother You; United Shades of America; Mudbound; How to Get Away with Murder; Scandal; The Cloverfield Paradox; Blindspotting; BlacKkKlansman; Little; If Beale Street Could Talk; Queen and Slim; A Black Lady Sketch Show

Dr Matt Jacobs *(PhD) is the Director of Wide Open Voices Ltd. He has 25 years' experience as a researcher, speaker, educator and organisational development specialist working with public, private and voluntary sector organisations who believe in social justice and equity.*

Lived experience: Zahra Bei, recovering teacher, PhD researcher and community organiser

As an educator, I had never come across the term 'Whiteness' up until 2016, nearly 20 years into the profession. Over my teaching career, all of which was in London, I have explored oppressions of many kinds, yet somehow the existence of Whiteness eluded me. I have been a secondary school teacher in one of the most diverse and unequal cities on the planet, the birthplace of empire, eugenics and racial order and yet utterly clueless about Whiteness. In my career, I have had the opportunity to have an impact on thousands of students and hundreds of colleagues, structures, policies and practices. As a pupil referral unit (PRU) teacher, a place where many children and young people excluded or at risk of exclusion from the mainstream can be found, I again failed to engage with Whiteness – the very nucleus of the 'race problem' (Leonardo, 2009), in spite of the PRU being a highly raced, classed, gendered and disabled setting, a space that disappears the educational other. I recognise that as being both my personal failure – as educators, we must actively and continuously seek critical knowledge – as well as a failure of at least two European education systems – in my case, the British and the Italian, both with deeply rooted White supremacist, colonial histories and makeups.

Whiteness was not included in my curriculum diet as an educator by the systems entrusted with my development, wellbeing and teacher training. If I hadn't taken a critical race studies module on my master's course almost 20 years in, it is very possible I would not be writing this. As an educator, I feel angry, cheated and deeply disappointed. In my case, Whiteness is also exceedingly personal. I am a woman of mixed heritage: Italian, Somali, Tanzanian, German. The colonial histories that explain how I have come to exist are not often pointed out but are nonetheless traceable.

I was born and raised in Rome, yet growing up I would routinely be asked the 'where are you from?' question. As a child, I was confused by that kind of question. (In his 1952 book *Black Skin, White Masks*, Frantz Fanon famously described this kind of European racialisation of Black people as 'exasperating'.) As I grew older, I could sense the 'exoticisation' sentiments. In my mind, I was the same as all my Italian friends and neighbours. I was a native. Over the years, I have been racialised as 'mixed-race', 'half-caste' or 'half breed', 'bi-racial', 'mulata', 'browning', 'meticcia'. Those are the politest ethnic descriptions. Mixed heritage is both a blessing and a curse (Du Bois, 1903; Leonardo, 2009). It gives you a unique window into privilege and Whiteness; it allows some membership to Blackness. But it never quite fits either bill entirely.

As an eight-year-old, I remember being frequently chased by some of my neighbours yelling, 'A n****, vattene al paese tuo!' ('Hey n*****, go back to your country!'). Even the Italian boy who later became my first boyfriend (and who ironically had much darker skin than me) called me 'n****' many times, as did other pupils. None of the Italian teachers who heard it ever challenged these children: racist name-calling was something to just live with. The 'normality' of racism that critical race theory illuminates (Gillborn, 2008) went unchecked. Italy felt monoculturally stifling, oppressive and repressive for a young girl of colour. I moved to London at the earliest opportunity, unaccompanied, at the age of 16. I was in search of belonging. As a pre-teen in the late 1980s, I would often watch Neneh Cherry's and Sade's music videos, and feel an affinity – at least an imaginary one – based on our shared mixed heritage. They looked like me! They were my first intersectional role models. I wanted to live somewhere where other people who looked like me belonged and thrived: this meant that so could I. It gave me hope and inspired me to take very bold steps, to escape my circumstances, which also included a tough home life.

By 16, I had started to notice other painful systems of oppression in my country of birth. Italian patriarchy is bold and unapologetic. It is deeply embedded right across society. I had also begun to notice endemic nepotism, still the norm to this day. I wanted no part of it and could have no part of it in any case since I come from a very working-class background and had virtually no social or economic capital at my disposal. I instinctively knew that as a young *ragazza esotica*, from a low-income, single-parent household, I had to do something drastic to improve my chances in life.

My first visit to London was cathartic. Experiencing the Notting Hill Carnival in 1991 was transformative; encountering Black bus drivers for the first time (I had only ever seen Black people as street sellers, sex workers or domestic help in Italy), and watching Sir Trevor McDonald on the six o'clock ITV News gave me hope. London seemed to me at that time, in the early nineties, to be a far more meritocratic and accepting space. In this place, difference was accepted, embraced and celebrated, not derided and marginalised or ignored. The 2016 Brexit referendum has markedly changed things. I have started to feel 'unwanted' once more, dislodged from the country I have tentatively come to call home. For the first time in a long while, I wonder about belonging again and am wrestling with the anxieties of alienation once more.

In all of this, Whiteness is pivotal in that it normalises the way we view the world, the way the world views us, the way we view ourselves and each other. Above all, Whiteness shapes the racialised expectations placed upon performative roles (Butler, 1990) of our socially prescribed identity categories. I had always thought my EU citizenship was a positive type of political and cultural identity. Now I am not so sure. Along with nearly three million EU migrants or 'others' living in Britain today, I awaited government announcements for five years that would determine whether or not, after 29 years, I could belong. And then there is the not-so-small matter of being an EU migrant of colour in Britain, with its own specificities, ambiguities and histories of dispossession. Lest we forget, Whiteness has 'the absolute right to exclude' (Gillborn, 2008).

Zahra Bei is a Black PhD student, trade unionist, community organiser and a former secondary school and pupil referral unit teacher, with 20 years in the classroom. Zahra is the founder of No More Exclusions (a national grassroots coalition movement in education) and co-founder of CARE2Liberate (Coalition of Anti-Racist Educators).

Summary

Key learning points

- Finding the right language to talk about race in schools empowers the next generation to become global citizens and to be better than the generations before them.
- Before you talk to students about race, take the time to gain some knowledge and understand the context, but don't let anxieties about 'getting things wrong' hold you back. The most important thing is making a start.
- Remember to listen to the opinions of those with lived experiences, don't make assumptions and don't take things personally. Be prepared to be uncomfortable and challenged.
- Language is power: it is only recently that conversations about Whiteness and White Privilege have become more commonplace. These conversations are important and need careful consideration. What can you do to disrupt Whiteness?

Key question

Whiteness, White Privilege, White gaze and White supremacy are all terms that are used with hesitancy. Is this language that you are comfortable using in a school context?

a) Absolutely, it is vital that these terms are used. They are embedded in our conversations and form part of our racial literacy.

b) Sometimes; however, it is dependent on the circumstance.

c) Rarely; it will be addressed if it is brought up.

d) Never; these terms make me feel very uncomfortable.

e) Hmm, what do they mean? I am not sure we should be using them.

Further self-reflection questions

1. How do we discuss the inclusion of others in the curriculum and in different areas of life without the White British community feeling fearful or feeling that their culture is being eroded?

2. How do we encourage White British people to see this as an opportunity to enrich their culture?
3. Whilst you are aware of Blackness, when did you learn about Whiteness? Do you think there is a reason for this distinction? Are we teaching our children that Whiteness is the standard and the norm?

Discussion points for staff meetings

- Do you think we should use the phrases 'White Privilege' and 'structural advantage or disadvantage' when talking to children and young people about race?
- Review your current policies. What language are you using when talking to children and young people about this topic?

6 Why are role models so important?

'How important it is for us to recognise and celebrate our heroes and she-roes.'
Maya Angelou

What is a role model?

How do you become a role model?

Do you need to be famous?

Should they look like you?

So many questions.

A role model is defined as 'a person looked to by others as an example to be imitated'. This definition from Oxford Dictionaries got me thinking. If a role model is to be imitated, then we really need to consider what we are demonstrating to our children. After all, they will be watching our every move.

During my teaching of PSHE, I always deliver a lesson on role models. We tend to look at prominent people in society and critique their roles. I ask students if they believe the person to be a role model and to consider what it takes to earn that title. Discussions include factors such as their contributions on social media and their status and impact in society, but most importantly, what the idea of role models means to the next generation.

A key theme that always comes up is the idea that once you are a role model, you are being watched. You set the standard, and children and young people copy everything you do. We see this in the new trend of influencers who suggest to us what we should watch, buy and wear. So, what happens when role models impact how a person views the world? When George Floyd was murdered on 25 May 2020, when protests began and when messages of solidarity flooded in, people were watching to see who posted black squares, who tweeted #BLM and who led protests and marches. In Bristol, protestors took down the statue of Colston which was in place in their city centre. This led to divided views. Some viewed the taking down of the statue as criminal. Others had the view that it was overdue activism. Who were the better role models? Those who petitioned peacefully or those who demanded to be heard?

Behaviour is an important aspect of modelling to our young people. Children and young people look to adults to confirm their views or challenge them. Children will always find role models and will take what is presented as the standard, the status quo. This is what will inform their understanding of stereotypes and the ideas that manifest in their minds.

Lived experience: Hardeep Singh Konsal, pastoral head of year

'When *Star Wars* came out, I was a kid. I remember the playground filled with children fighting with sticks like lightsabres, saying in their deepest prepubescent voices, 'I am your father!'. I have to admit, I didn't get it. However, unbeknownst to me, I wouldn't understand what all the fuss was about until decades later when *Black Panther* hit the cinemas – and I would go to see it ten times!' (Sabrina Bramble, 2020)

When a young boy or girl isn't represented well or at all, it can lead to a decrease in self-confidence or a tendency to learn and accept the stereotypes laid out for them. We need representation of all ethnicities with all different personality types instead of just one static stereotype (angry/ghetto Black girl, gangster/violent Black man, Asian shopkeeper/honour killings).

I was blessed. In my personal life I had my uncle and my Sikh faith to provide vital role models and values. My uncle influenced many people by giving guidance on being a better person; he was always there to lend a helping hand. He put others' needs before his own. He was just someone I looked up to; he taught me to be who I am today, and without a beautiful role model and friend like my uncle, I wouldn't have the opportunities that I have today. He has inspired me to be a better person: to never give up, to keep your head above water and to enjoy life while you can. He always taught me to stay positive, not focus on negative energy, and most importantly to be myself – no matter what anyone thinks.

What happens if you don't have a role model in your personal life? Education may be the only place that a young person or child has the opportunity to find a role model. It's empowering for young people to see others like themselves in a variety of roles, and it's also educational for other groups who may be unfamiliar with a specific demographic of people. I ask you, what are you doing to inspire a young person? What support is needed within your own community? Young people often look for role models within their families and communities. However, they can get influenced and trapped into following the wrong types of role models.

'There is something that may be even more important than Black students having Black teachers, and that is White students having Black teachers.' Gloria Ladson-Billings (2018)

Looking into the past, the school I was educated in was predominately White British with no representation of ethnic minorities. Racial incidents were commonplace, which was compounded by the fact that I had no role models or adults in my education setting I could connect with. The lack of empathy and sympathy in these scenarios made me feel angry and anxious. I also felt unstable in some situations – particularly those where I felt I was held back. This is why my career in education has led me to focus on bringing positive change and support for diverse communities.

In 2014, Octavia Spencer spoke about the importance of what's known in the film and television industry as 'colour-blind casting': 'Little kids need to be able to turn on the TV and see real-world representations of themselves. It's very important. You need that representation.' Spencer said she would like to see decisions based on 'the best actor for the part', adding: 'Who cares if the lead is an Asian male? If this is the best actor for that role, why does the role have to be indicative of a person's ethnicity?' Role models are essential. They help us become the person we want to be and inspire us to make a difference. Choosing a role model wisely means that you are influenced correctly and that you can become the best person you can be. I never had any role models while I was in school or in a workplace setting. I had idols I admired within the entertainment world, people like Ian Wright, Bruce Lee and Apache Indian (he was the only person I saw on mainstream TV who looked like me or came close to representing me). But they all occupied a space far away from me; they were not my school teachers, nor were they my employers or people I could talk to for support.

In my professional life, whether it be in education or employment, I never saw anyone and thought, 'Yes, I would like to be like them' or 'That person represents me.' I have been to many training courses designed for 'BAME people', where I've been buddied up with a White, middle-class mentor or role model. A lot of them have been good. However, they never represented me. They could never understand my struggles and how difficult it can be for someone coming from a South Asian background.

Having one positive role model in school could make a massive difference to a young person. They'll probably be more likely to finish school, as well as being more successful in the world of work. Representation in professional settings is essential to ensure that these children have role models to base themselves on.

I made a difference. How do I know? Young people keep coming back to me to tell me so, after they have finished college, or after they've graduated from university and are working or having families of their own. I never support them for personal gain. I wanted them to learn what they needed to learn and help them better themselves to become role models to others.

Hardeep Singh Konsal is a pastoral head of year. He is a committed and dedicated champion of the disadvantaged, working tirelessly with young people, facilitating change and enabling them to take a full and active part within their own education.

Finding the *right* role models

We often hear the phrase, 'You can't be what you can't see', which has become a bit of a cliché. I certainly hope that this is not true – as this is often the experience of our Black, Asian and racially minoritised children. Perhaps this would explain why many Black, Asian and racially minoritised people continue to be underrepresented in a variety of professions – they are not seeing themselves represented in the world. As referenced in my 2019 TEDx Bristol talk, 'Why representation really matters': 'All the representation I see is White men in authority.' Therefore, if White middle-class men are the norm and the status quo, it is easy to see why Black, Asian and racially minoritised children and young people feel like they do not belong in certain spaces or struggle to visualise themselves in different roles. This does not mean that Black, Asian and racially minoritised people do not take a variety of career paths, but the figures across most professions show that they remain underrepresented.

I grew up seeing very little representation in my life. Seeing a Black person who looked like me – in roles or places that interested me – was a very rare occurrence. Role models became people I would never meet: celebrities or deceased icons. However, as an adult, it became quite clear to me that I had got this all wrong. Role models are everywhere. They are you and me. There is always a child watching and waiting to hear and see what we do. Our everyday actions are being imitated and we are influencing the minds of the next generation. When I was mentoring for a charity some years ago, the conversations regarding role models were common. Yet I don't think we had a full appreciation for what it meant and what it is that we need to demonstrate to a young person. If a young man can challenge me by saying that the only representation of himself was in sport, media or crime, I must ask the question: who were his role models? There are so many potential role models for children in every aspect of their lives, but we must make sure they are surrounded in real life by role models who are authentic and who understand the influence they have over young minds.

Research has shown that a Black student is more likely to feel like they belong in their chosen field if they have had access to Black role models (see, for example, Universities UK, 2019, and Funk and Parker, 2018). This is one of the reasons that the commitment to improving the lack of diversity in education has been supported by the Department for Education. It is believed that the experiences of Black, Asian and minoritised children would improve and their potential achievements would increase if they had a teacher or mentor who looked like them. Reasons cited have included that students felt that they didn't have to explain themselves, they felt a sense of connection and identity, and they also felt that they would be treated more fairly. The benefits for Black, Asian and minoritised children are clear, but what does this role modelling do for White children? It is beneficial for them also. It's important for White children to see people of other ethnicities in positions of authority. By creating more equitable representation within education, we move towards providing a global perspective – as opposed to a Eurocentric colonial view of superiority.

Activity: Who are your role models?

List ten people you would deem to be a role model. Consider the identity markers that are attached to these individuals and then answer the following questions:

1. Do you spot any trends, traits or characteristics related to these individuals?
2. Are you able to identify role models you connect with physically, emotionally and spiritually?
3. Are the role models selected professionally affiliated or personal?
4. Do you see yourself as a role model?

Educational role models are important. What children see and hear from early childhood development all the way through to adolescence is crucial. It will ultimately shape who they are and who they become. When you consider that during this period, children spend over 700 hours per year with teachers, it's easy to see how the ideas, messaging and role modelling of teachers make such a difference to the ideologies that a child ultimately develops.

Lived experience: Kemi Oloyede, educator and founder of the Young Black Teachers Network

It's period five on a Wednesday (hump day) and I'm looking forward to the school day ending. My classroom is silent as Year 11 students are working on exam questions. So quiet you could hear a pin drop, which is very unusual in a PRU setting.

Student:	*Miss?*
Me:	*Yes, [insert name here].*
Student:	*I just want to say thank you for being a good teacher. I hated science before I came here, but now I'm actually learning.*
Me:	*(Holding back the tears) Thank you for saying that.*

After the lesson, I spoke to the student about his experiences of science in his previous mainstream setting. He told me that he'd never had a Black science teacher and that he didn't even know Black women could be science teachers. I was shocked to hear this, as it was 2019 and I didn't think I'd be having this kind of conversation, but this is the reality for a lot of students.

I started my teaching career in 2013 and I knew I wanted to make a difference to the lives of the children I taught, but for some reason what this student said hit me in a different way. That's when I realised: I'm not a role model. I am a real model.

Being a role model means playing or acting. As if once the school bell rings, I will become a different person from the one students see and know. This didn't sit well with me. I believe in being authentic and bringing your authentic self to the classroom every day because that's what children need, especially in this day and age, when social media is so prolific. 'Authentic' and 'real' go hand in hand, and students can see right through you when you're acting.

Being a real model means I bring my most faithful and best self forward each and every time I stand before my students because I can only expect from them what I'm willing to do myself. Since the first day I started teaching, I committed to my students and myself to be the person they need me to be and the person I needed when I was a student. Don't get me wrong, I had great teachers when I was growing up who were good at their jobs, and a few who left a lasting impact on me, but I didn't see past the role they were paid to inhabit – teaching.

Teachers are overworked, and Covid-19 has shown me just how undervalued we are. When I feel like I want to leave the profession, I remember my 'why?' and my personal definition of a real model. I will teach you about homeostasis and the periodic table and I will also be real with you about life and prepare you for that by leading by example. I will encourage you to be bold and stand up for what is right, and I will also tell you when you're wrong and how to treat others with respect. I don't sugar coat, but I am gentle. I am not harsh, but I am firm. My expectations and standards are high because I want the best from you and for you. I will not spoon-feed you, but I will guide you in making the right decisions for yourself. I will protect you, but I will also expose you to extraordinary opportunities that will shape your future and give you a chance of being more than you could ever have imagined for yourself.

Growing up, I heard a lot of adults say, 'Do as I say, not as I do.' And that is wrong in my eyes, especially now that I am a teacher. I leave an imprint on my students, and I always want that imprint to be a positive one. I am not a mother yet, but I see my students as my children. I believe I have a duty as a Black woman and as a teacher whose students are mainly Black to show up for my students and be as real as real can be in the most loving way. I must plant a seed of authenticity into each student, water that seed and allow it to grow in the hope that they will one day do the same for another child.

Kemi Oloyede is the founder of the Young Black Teachers Network, an educational consultant, SENCO and science teacher. Kemi is using her platform to support fellow Black teachers in the education sector and to increase the number of Black teachers in education and progress into leadership.

Role models and racism

In the UEFA EURO 2020 men's football final, Bukayo Saka, Jadon Sancho and Marcus Rashford all missed their penalties. Three young Black men. They had put themselves forward to represent England and lead as role models for us all. Yet the admiration, inspiration and imitation was lost for some the moment they missed their penalties. So, what does it really mean to be a role model? Is it conditional? Is it subject to success? Those three Black men, within minutes of the match ending, were engulfed in a negative pool of racism from angry fans. The hate they received took place across many platforms. What role modelling did this demonstrate to our children and young people? What happens when a role model demonstrates racist or discriminatory behaviour? Can our children and young people separate the person from the behaviour or is it as the definition says? Do they simply imitate?

I recently heard a parent having a conversation about her child's experience of witnessing the horrific football racism online. The parent talked about how she explained to her child how to report racism and discrimination online. By doing this, the parent equipped their child with an understanding of what a racist incident is and discussed the ways in which it can be challenged at school and in personal settings. The parent also gave her child the chance to express their emotion and thoughts. This is what positive role modelling is about. So, think about how you would model a challenge to a child and what steps you would take if a child in your care had witnessed racism.

Summary

Key learning points

- Role models are everywhere. Children imitate the everyday actions of adults and adults influence the minds of the next generation. It's important that we surround children with positive role models and are also aware of our own actions as educators. We have a responsibility to model the behaviour we want to see.
- When Black, Asian and racially minoritised children have role models who look like them, they are more likely to feel a sense of belonging in certain spaces and visualise themselves in different roles.
- Positive role models are essential when it comes to tackling racism. Positive role models will support children in challenging racism and give them a chance to express their emotion and thoughts.

Key question

Do you think it is important to have role models who look like you and have the same culture, heritage or background?

a) Yes

b) No

c) Sometimes

How does this support the notion of representation?

Further self-reflection questions

1. Who and what are you representing when you step into the classroom?
2. What kind of seed are you planting in the lives of the next generation?
3. Who do you want to help?

4. Why do you want to make a difference?
5. What will you be doing in order to achieve this?
6. Can you be the positive role model children need?

Discussion points for staff meetings

- The responsibility of a role model is great, but is it fair to say that they are merely acting or holding a position?
- What does it mean to be a real model? Does it involve the real you showing up or are you playing a role?

PART 3

Creating an action plan

7 The legal framework

'Tell me and I will forget. Show me and I may remember. Involve me and I learn.'
Benjamin Franklin

Over a decade ago, the British government introduced the Equality Act 2010. The Act was designed to be a single piece of legislation that legally protects people from discrimination in workplaces, schools and other areas of society. The Act covers nine 'protected characteristics' and states that it is against the law to discriminate against anyone because they have one or more of these protected characteristics. Race, including colour, nationality, and ethnic and national origin, is one of those characteristics. The Act outlines the public sector duty that schools need to adhere to in relation to these nine characteristics.

Often when I meet with clients to discuss their needs, they will ask that staff receive a basic understanding of the law that is applicable to educators. This is usually covered as part of an initial induction for new teachers or as part of annual equity, diversity and inclusion training. So, what do you know already?

Activity

What are the nine protected characteristics covered by the Equality Act 2010? Try listing them out below.

What are the three duties that schools must uphold?

1.

2.

3.

What policies are in place in your school in regard to the Equality Act 2010?

In my experience, most educators can name seven out of nine of the protected characteristics covered by the Equality Act 2010. The full list is as follows:

1. age
2. gender reassignment
3. being married or in a civil partnership
4. being pregnant or on maternity leave
5. disability
6. race
7. religion or belief
8. sex
9. sexual orientation.

So far, so good. However, when it comes to answering the second and third questions, which relate to how the Equality Act 2010 applies to their school, educators often struggle.

The three duties that schools must uphold are as follows:

1. Eliminate discrimination, harassment, victimisation and other conduct that is prohibited by the Equality Act 2010.
2. Advance equality of opportunity between people who share a protected characteristic and people who do not share it.
3. Foster good relations across all protected characteristics – between people who share a protected characteristic and people who do not share it.

It is common for policy to be used as a means of implementing the Equality Act 2010. Here are some examples of policies in schools that may speak to its existence:

- equality policy
- child-friendly equality policy
- equality statement
- equality objectives on the website.

So, what is the use of the Equality Act 2010 in the context of our schools if most educators are aware that it exists but do not know how it applies to their school? How does this help schools achieve anti-racist practice? The truth is that it doesn't and it won't, if used in isolation. The problem with the Equality Act 2010 is that it has simply become another tick-box piece of legislation that normalises compliance and does little to enforce the change needed in our current times. It has provided a more palatable version of challenge and no longer forces the explicit demonisation of racism.

Applying the legal framework in a more meaningful way

In order to ensure the Equality Act 2010 is being applied, all schools should ensure they have the following as a minimum requirement:

- equality, diversity, and inclusion (EDI) policy, which is available on the school website
- equality statement
- equality objectives that are reported on annually and updated every three years
- relationships and sex education (RSE) policy, with specific reference to PSHE delivery and teaching related to LGBTQIA+ communities
- a completed equality impact assessment on all school policies.

However, policies will only go so far in upholding the duties of the Equality Act 2010. Eliminating discrimination, advancing equality of opportunity and fostering good relations requires much more than a commitment to doing so on paper. When you start considering the law and its application in your school, you will realise quite quickly that it is not as straightforward as you might think. For example, how do we ensure there is space for intersectionality and different versions of truth? What happens if a person's religious beliefs mean that they struggle to support LGBTQIA+ communities? How do you foster 'good relationships' between these two groups? How do you ensure that both groups feel a sense of connection and belonging?

The truth is that each individual school must consider how the protected characteristics manifest themselves in their unique setting. Where do they intersect and where might they conflict? Remember, you may not be able to pigeon-hole all groups or all individuals neatly under one protected characteristic. Intersectionality means that certain groups or individuals will have very specific challenges and therefore very specific needs. How do you take this into account? How do you communicate with these groups and with individuals to ascertain how you can best serve them?

Ultimately, having a deep knowledge about the communities you serve, listening to their views, and formulating unique policies and action plans to support their needs is the way forward. This may be much more complex and time-consuming than writing a one-size-fits-all EDI policy, but it will ensure your school is applying the legal framework in a meaningful way.

British values

A few years after the introduction of the Equality Act 2010, we saw the introduction of 'British values' in schools. In 2014, the Department for Education published guidance on 'promoting' these values in schools 'to ensure young people leave school prepared for life in modern Britain' (Department for Education, 2014c). This was quickly woven into PSHE and humanities subjects, which were treated as a place for these values to call home.

Activity

Can you name the four British values?

1.

2.

3.

4.

How did you get on with the activity above? The answer is that the four British values are identified as follows:

- democracy
- the rule of law
- individual liberty
- mutual respect for and tolerance of those with different faiths and beliefs, and for those without faith.

But what does the teaching of such values mean? After all, what does it mean to be British? Samara Cameron, who took the lead on teaching British values in her school, will explore this further in her lived experience piece.

Lived experience: Samara Cameron, SEN class teacher

My understanding of how British values became an agenda in 2014 is that documentation appeared that alleged extremism from the Islamic State, which, it was claimed, had planned to groom young people in Birmingham schools (Shackle, 2017). Although the alleged plot to groom young people was in fact disproven, this was enough to launch investigations, government reports and reform for British values in the education system. British values are mentioned in other educational literature, however from 2014 the emphasis was that schools needed to strategise and implement British values within their school improvement plans.

I was asked by my headteacher if I could take the lead on executing this in the school. Prior to going on any training, I regretted the examples I had seen schools promoting as their British values. Fish and chips, the Queen, cups of tea and the Union Jack – all examples on displays of how schools were now interpreting what British values meant to them. It was incredibly interesting because none of those so-called British examples resonated with me. My British values looked incredibly different, especially as a Black British woman who was raised by Jamaican parents. At that point I realised that the job at hand was much larger than I had imagined. The context of my school was 98 per cent minority ethnic and a high proportion of students were Muslim and my task was unpicking how to embed these ideas for third-generation children of immigrants.

Firstly, I wanted to focus on why extremism groups targeted young people, in particular young People of Colour. Having listened to the stories of young people who turned to extremism or were groomed, it is clear to see that a lot of the reasons they were open to this were due to wanting a community to belong to. The young people chosen for this process are often those from disadvantaged contexts, who feel disenfranchised, feel unable to be heard and are longing for an identity. Youngsters also look to people who look like themselves because they are familiar. This is why representation is so crucial. What young people can envision gives them a goal or aspiration to achieve what they can see. This is also why influencers have such a huge responsibility because the digitisation of our society now means people can be reached globally incredibly quickly.

Secondly, I refused to use the stereotypes of what was considered traditional British symbolism, like red post boxes and red double-decker buses. I also resented the fact that I knew a lot of what I needed to do to prove implementation was to tick all the metaphorical boxes. My aim went beyond box-ticking: it was to address the need of identity and to enrich the children's understanding of who they are in the context of the world around them.

'British values' is the overarching title for the four main categories that make British values what they are: democracy, rule of law, individual liberty, and mutual respect and tolerance of those with different faiths and beliefs – and for those without faith (Young Citizens). Considering my personal context, the values I concentrated on mainly were mutual respect and tolerance. Embedding democracy, rule of law and individual liberty within our curriculum was quite manageable because, in my opinion, they are quite well defined. However, teaching mutual respect and tolerance was far more challenging because I realised not only did the children need to understand what this looked like, but my fellow colleagues and their parents needed to be taught also.

A lot of the issues with British values do not relate to knowledge and understanding of them. The real struggle is executing them daily, as core beliefs that each person should have. Being a Black educator, I felt an extreme pressure to have to demonstrate these values articulately for the children to appreciate. I remember vividly a Black child asking me why I spoke to a member of management (a Caucasian woman) because the child thought she was rude. What a wonderful opportunity to demonstrate the depth of character and the choices that we need to make daily to navigate in life as Black people.

My learning from having the British values role gave me some life lessons. First, being a role model does not mean perfection, but our children need a plethora of good role models and positive representations of Black people. This should never be isolated to musicians and athletes, which I had to campaign against in my context during Black History Month in 2016. Secondly, we need our school leaders to continue to make Black history a priority on their agendas. The role of British values lead in my school was diminished in 2018 when they had Ofsted in and they passed outstandingly in that area. However, it is difficult to maintain excellence if you haven't got somebody driving it forward and adapting it to the changes that life brings. Lastly, if we do not make efforts to change the way Black people are represented in education, then how do we reform? We need to cultivate our young People of Colour so they can be equipped to be able to make informed decisions. To decide to be respectful to a police officer even though you know it is an unjust stop and search has to have been embedded deep down within that individual long before the incident takes place.

Samara Cameron is a passionate experienced teacher who has taught in various boroughs and has covered all year groups of the primary sector. Currently, Samara is a primary SEN teacher.

Additional principles and guidance to consider

When we think about the context in which anti-discrimination and anti-racist practice sits and the frameworks we use, we have to go beyond the legislation in the Equality Act 2010 and the Department for Education's guidance on British values. We must consider other principles and guidance that govern education:

- Promoting Fundamental British Values as Part of SMSC (Spiritual, Moral, Social and Cultural Development) in Schools 2014
- Counter Terrorism and Security Act 2015
- The Prevent Agenda
- The UN Convention on the Rights of the Child
- Keeping Children Safe in Education
- Human Rights Act 1998
- Working Together to Safeguard Children
- Duty to Report Female Genital Mutilation 2015
- RSE Statutory Guidance 2020

All classroom teachers should have a working knowledge and understanding of at least three of these pieces of legislation: Keeping Children Safe in Education, Working Together to Safeguard Children and the Prevent Agenda. The Teachers' Standards form another key piece of documentation that early career teachers and their mentors must be aware of and this will be explored further in Chapter 8. However, in my opinion, every teacher should familiarise themselves with all of the above guidance, especially if they are going to take an active role in diversity, equity and inclusion within their practice, department or school. It is also important to consider this guidance and how it is being implemented through a critical lens. How are these frameworks serving the children and young people in your school? How biased are they? Are particular groups disproportionately affected by the impact of these documents?

Summary

Key learning points

- It's not enough to have a basic knowledge of the Equality Act 2010 and the protected characteristics it covers. All school staff need to have a clear understanding of how this legislation applies in their setting and the steps they are accountable for taking.

- British values do not look the same for everyone. Think about what 'being British' looks like in the context of your school and the lives of your students. Tailor your teaching of these values accordingly.
- There are a number of other principles and guidelines that need to be considered through the lens of anti-discrimination and anti-racist practice. Schools need to think about whether they truly serve the students in their care.

Key question

Are British values embedded in your school?

a) Yes
b) Somewhat
c) Via PSHE only
d) Nope!

Further self-reflection questions

1. What do we mean when we say we are being 'tolerant'? Is it an appropriate term to use when talking about inclusivity?
2. What does the 'rule of law' mean?
3. What does it mean to have 'individual liberty'?
4. Is living in a democracy causing the UK to lose control of 'free speech'?
5. What does being British mean to you and your student population?
6. Can British values incite further division?

Discussion points for staff meetings

- What does being British mean to your school?
- Ask your staff and the children in your school the same question. Consider the answers as a staff team and assess what steps are needed to further explore British identity and what it means in the twenty-first century. For younger children, ask them to use pictures and imagery to explore what they think it means to be British.

8 Teacher training

'Every child deserves a champion: an adult who will never give up on them, who understands the power of connection and insists they become the best they can possibly be.'

Rita Pierson (2013)

I never thought I would be an assistant principal. I tried to stay as far away as possible from education – or rather taking up education as a profession, vocation or career choice. I didn't have the best school experience and I had no interest in going back there.

I spent most of my teenage years feeling like I was on the other side of the glass box. My educational experience represented exclusion and othering. The words still ring in my ears, 'Here comes trouble.' I wondered what I'd done to deserve that title. As an adult I reflect on those years and I realise how much they shaped me. They trained me. They prepared me for a world of racism that I had no idea I was about to encounter.

As a trained primary teacher, my mum tried for years to convince me to transition into education. She felt that I would make a good teacher. I'm not sure if it was the fact that I liked to talk or that I liked to command a room, but whatever she saw in me, she felt there was something I had to offer the next generation. But me being me, I was stubborn and kept saying no. After all, what did I have to teach? What could I share? Who would listen to me?

As I mentioned in Chapter 1, I attended a mono-cultural secondary school where most of the student population was White British. Whilst the students were not necessarily local to the school and the intake came from across the city, White British was still the dominant community in our school. At the time, my mum thought that this was the best place for me. She wanted me to attend a school where I would not be with my local peers (code for: people who looked like me). But what my mum didn't realise in making that decision was that I would go to a school where I was alone. She wanted me to focus on my education and achieve great results. Academically I did OK, but what I failed at – or certainly felt I failed at – was understanding myself.

I felt that I had a double consciousness. The version of Aisha that was bussed out of Bristol to South Gloucestershire and the version of Aisha that came back to Easton in Bristol. This created the most excruciating tug-of-war in my mind. I often think of that bus journey as a shapeshifter process. I removed my Blackness to become palatable to my White teachers and White peers. On the journey home, I Blacked up again, ready for home, ready to reconnect with my local community. But somehow, I never got this right. I felt like an outsider no matter where I was. I went through the trauma of 'You are too Black for us' and 'You are not Black enough for us'. I remember hearing my mum get upset when people would make comments about me: 'Her daughter thinks she is nice.' They called my mum a 'coconut'. They said she thought her children were better than the other children and this was shown in the school that she had chosen for me. I just wanted to be accepted.

I often think about the teachers I had at school. I think about my science teacher, the one Black teacher in my educational experience. Although she was my chemistry teacher and I saw her regularly, we didn't have a close relationship. In fact, I felt that she intentionally distanced herself from me. Well, that was certainly my interpretation. I sometimes wondered what thoughts went through her head. Did she feel that it was her responsibility to be the Black spokesperson for the Black children in our school? Or did she avoid it, as it wasn't her job to do that? I sometimes question how other staff felt about her. Was she the token Black teacher in the school? Would she be expected to support us or tell us off when the handful of us needed sorting out?

Teacher training should prepare trainees for all aspects of what they may experience during their teacher training year, in the hope that the skills and tools that they gain will support them as they continue with their career. Yet, the one aspect of teacher training that is rarely covered is information about equality, diversity and inclusion. Some courses will have a unit that covers refugees, asylum seekers and students who speak English as an additional language. But that is rare. Therefore, the idea of a trainee teacher receiving training in regard to anti-racist practice is almost unheard of. My mum says that in her teacher training, she was taught how to deal with pupils and racism, but not how to deal with adults and racism. They did have some initiatives as teachers, but they were focused on how to welcome children from different cultures, rather than empowering children to see difference.

Nevertheless, with a more diverse population of students and an ever-changing workforce, there is now pressure on schools to do more to diversify and decolonise their curriculum. How is this possible if they never received adequate training? In 2021, it was announced that all students on hair and beauty courses would now receive mandatory training on Afro-Caribbean hair. In Wales, they announced that the teaching of Black history would be mandatory in all schools. It is clear that there is now a movement dedicated to empowering learners and ensuring that they are more equipped. But what about teachers?

Lived experience: Shauna Stewart, head of department and teacher of secondary education

When the opportunity to contribute to this book arose, the seeds of doubt that I have fought my entire life started to creep back in. What could I possibly say that has any value? Why would anyone want to read anything that I had written? It was those questions, those seeds of doubt, that made me realise these were the exact reasons why I needed to contribute. I am confident that those questions are asked amongst many young Black children who doubt their place in the world, their abilities, whether they can achieve success and whether they are good enough.

All teachers are shaped by their own experience of education. We remember our favourite teachers and we recognise our least favourite – not always by name but definitely by how they made us feel.

I was fortunate enough to attend a primary school that was diverse in its cohort; there were children from all religions, backgrounds and walks of life. To name one example, I remember welcoming children from Montserrat who had to flee their beautiful home due to a devastating volcanic eruption. The staff at my primary school were not diverse. All the teaching staff were female, and almost all were White. Even though the staff body did not reflect the community it served, I saw some great teaching practices that helped to promote inclusivity. More than that, we were taught to celebrate the things that made us different.

This Church of England primary school taught us about Diwali, provided us with the opportunity to make lanterns and decorate our classrooms to celebrate the Hindu and Sikh festival of light, took us to visit mosques in the local community, and lots more – whilst still maintaining its core Christian values. This Church of England primary school encouraged us to stand tall and educate our peers about our own cultural and religious practices and it was through this peer-led interaction that I learnt so much about my Rastafarian, Muslim, Christian, Sikh, Black, White and Brown classmates.

When training to teach and reflecting on my own experiences, this nourishing time in my school life was so important. I realised that perhaps my teachers did not know about the different cultures in their classrooms but that did not make them shy away from embracing them. They used our own self-pride not only as a way to build our confidence and educate our peers but also as a way to educate themselves.

My primary school experience taught me how we should be celebrated in the classroom and it's something I have always held on to throughout my career; it is also something that has been consistently challenged.

Secondary school is a big transition for all students; the small and familial setting of primary school is swapped for the enormous hustle and bustle of secondary school life, which can be daunting. It was this transition that made me acutely aware of my racial difference. I did not see myself at secondary school, neither amongst my peers nor my teachers. At first, I was OK with that; I thought that just like primary school, I would have the opportunity to share who I was with pride and be celebrated for being different. I thought wrong.

Racism flowed through the classrooms, the corridors and the playground with ease – 'Oh, I don't like saying the word "Black" because it's not a good word, so I'll just refer to you as "coloured"'; 'Oh, I bought it from the P*** shop down the road.' My job at school became to educate my friends and peers on why this was wrong. Should it have been my job? No. Why was it my job? Because no one else was doing it.

A key moment in my secondary school life came when I had to challenge a teacher on her own racism. I was 12 at the time and we were reading a text which contained the N-word. Every time the word came up, 29 pairs of eyes would look at me. I was a very confident 12-year-old, and I was OK with this, as I knew we were reading a book and my peers were looking at me from a place of discomfort. Upon reflection, I always think about how a different, less confident, less self-assured Black 12-year-old may have felt in that situation and how let down they would have felt when the room's authority, the class teacher, did nothing to address the discomfort.

In this same class, we were asked to design a poster advertising a slave auction. I refused. My less articulate 12-year-old self explained that I would never create a poster promoting the disgusting treatment of my ancestors. I was removed from the room and sanctioned for disruptive behaviour and refusal to follow instructions. When I challenged this, I was permanently moved to a different class and the matter was never discussed again. When I think back to this time, I wonder if the class teacher ever learned anything from my reaction. Did this make them rethink their teaching practice, or was I labelled as a disruptive Black girl pulling the race card?

During the early part of my teaching career, I found myself in another situation where I had to stand up to authority and defend my race. A senior leadership team member challenged my professional dress citing that my colourful headscarves looked more like I was coming to 'wash clothes rather than to teach'. I was outrageously offended and angered by this comment. Nothing during my teacher training had prepared me for anything like this; in fact, race was never discussed. Despite being unprepared for such an encounter in my professional career, I did what many of us as Black professionals do: I suppressed my raw emotion for fear of being labelled as an angry Black woman. Instead I sought to teach my superior about how insensitive and offensive their comment was and offered an opportunity for them to have an open conversation, with a view to eradicating the ignorance they had shown my culture and my pride. This offer was never accepted. After some persistence from myself, a written apology was issued and the matter was never raised again. Once again, I found myself in a situation where a White teacher's opportunity to learn about their missteps as a professional, from someone's personal experience, someone whom they had wronged, was missed.

Many schools use the concept of restorative justice as a way for children and young people to learn how their behaviour impacts others and serves as a structured opportunity for growth – the same could and should be applied as part of our reflective practice as professionals.

Shauna Stewart has taught in mainstream schools and pupil referral units, and has a background in youth work and in working in social care regarding educational outcomes for children in foster care.

Reflective practice

When I reflect on the last few years, I see so much privilege and honour in my role as an assistant principal. I will often open my talks with the phrase, 'There is no better profession in the world than being an educator. We teach everyone something.' Yet I question if we all have the same commitment to educating children. How can we if we are not committed to ensuring that *all* children are included and not subjected to the feeling or experience of othering?

As educators, we are very focused on the experience of the learner. However, we have to be willing to learn, unlearn, adapt and change too. Some of the most difficult but effective learning happens in getting it wrong; we need to be aware of our thought processes and be willing to hold the mirror up to ourselves to understand what it is that we need to do in order to change and improve. Another part of this process should be that we as individuals are willing to apologise for our role in causing upset or potentially triggering trauma for the other party. We also need to be willing to understand that they might not accept that apology. This process should form part of our ongoing reflective practice throughout our careers as educators.

As Shauna mentions in her lived experience piece, the increasingly popular concept of restorative justice could be used as a tool for educators to address their own behaviour in relation to race as part of their reflective practice as professionals. To put this into practice, think about how your behaviour may have impacted on an individual pupil, a group of pupils in your class, or even a colleague. For example, you could consider a specific moment when you acted in a certain way, used a certain word or phrase, misinterpreted a child's viewpoint or lived experience, or simply could have handled things in a different way. It could be something you were called out for at the time or something you did that you now realise was problematic, since having done some additional work and learning.

Without becoming defensive or trying to justify your actions, take a moment to think deeply about the pupil's (or colleague's) experience and how your behaviour may have impacted them. If it's appropriate and you are sure it won't cause further damage, talk to the child (or colleague) about it, acknowledging that you were in the wrong, apologising and listening carefully to what they have to say. Now think about what you would do differently next time, write it down and make a commitment to act on it.

In these cases, it's important not to fixate on the fact that you didn't mean to cause any harm but instead create space and acknowledge that the impact of your actions may have outweighed what you intended to do. Emily Meadows, a LGBTQ+ consultant for international schools, and Daniel Wickner, who delivers diversity, equity, inclusion and justice work in schools, explain that focusing on 'intent' centres the feelings of White people, whereas focusing on possible impact centres the feelings of People of Colour. For a deeper understanding of intent versus impact, read this interview with Emily and Daniel and take a look at their resources: www.tieonline.com/article/2830/antiracism-intent-vs-impact.

Initial teacher training

Since the summer of 2020, the discussion regarding race and racism has made it back on to the agenda. Schools have been very keen to look at their inclusive practice, in particular their anti-racist practice. There isn't a school in the country that isn't debating it. Equalities leads are busy considering what they should add to their CPD or annual training package. But if we are to truly make a change, training cannot simply be an e-module once a year or form part of the annual September INSET day. Yet for most, this is all it will be. What I'm interested in is taking it back further and examining what it is we are training our teachers to do in the first place. What is in their toolkit when they arrive fresh-faced and ready to teach?

The Teachers' Standards

Let's start with the Teachers' Standards.

Trainees are expected to provide evidence of the impact of their teaching upon pupil progress over time. The intention is that trainees will create evidence bundles to support a more holistic approach in evaluating their progress over the year. The following excerpts taken from the Teachers' Standards in England (Department for Education, 2021d) highlight some important phrases which are crucial to anti-racist education. I analysed these standards and my question is this: when trainees see these standards, do they ever view them through the lens of race? Do they go through an equality impact assessment and ensure that the needs of all children, irrespective of their cultural heritage or background, are met with the highest standard? Or do they just accept the status quo?

Part one: Teaching

A teacher must…

'1. Set high expectations which inspire, motivate and challenge pupils' and 'establish a safe and stimulating environment for pupils, rooted in mutual respect'

Reality: Black Caribbean and Gypsy, Roma and Traveller children continue to be excluded at a rate that is disproportionate to White children (Department for Education, 2020a).

'2. Promote good progress and outcomes by pupils'

Reality: Educational attainment gaps continue to exist, in particular between Black Caribbean and Gypsy, Roma and Traveller children, and their White peers. Black Caribbean students are 11 months behind on average. Gypsy, Roma and Traveller children are almost three years behind on average (Bhopal, 2018).

'3. Demonstrate good subject and curriculum knowledge'

Reality: Many teachers struggle to take account of Black British history and British Asian history in their subject areas. Typically, humanities subjects such as history will look to slavery, British Empire and colonialism as areas of study. Yet teachers struggle to diversify the curriculum beyond this and ensure that more equitable representation is evident in their curriculum and lesson design.

'5. Adapt teaching to respond to the strengths and needs of all pupils' and 'have a clear understanding of the needs of all pupils, including... those with English as an additional language'

Reality: Many children with English as an additional language (EAL) are treated as second-class citizens, a nuisance and a difficulty beyond differentiation. These children are often placed in sets of lower ability and grouped with children who have behavioural needs. Resources and access to a comprehensive EAL programme are limited.

Part two: Personal and professional conduct

'Teachers uphold public trust in the profession and maintain high standards of ethics and behaviour, within and outside school, by:

- *treating pupils with dignity, building relationships rooted in mutual respect, and at all times observing proper boundaries appropriate to a teacher's professional position*
- *having regard for the need to safeguard pupils' well-being, in accordance with statutory provisions*
- *showing tolerance of and respect for the rights of others*
- *not undermining fundamental British values, including democracy, the rule of law, individual liberty and mutual respect, and tolerance of those with different faiths and beliefs*
- *ensuring that personal beliefs are not expressed in ways which exploit pupils' vulnerability or might lead them to break the law.'*

Reality: But what does it mean not to undermine British values? In the twenty-first century, what does it mean to be British?

Question

Can trainees and educators state that they are truly meeting the Teachers' Standards if Black and other children of colour continue to fail in the current system?

Anti-racist practice as part of initial teacher training

The current QTS (qualified teacher status) does not require a commitment to anti-racist practice – and there is no requirement for this during your PGCE training. While most providers will include a unit on inclusion, what is taught and how it is taught is subject to the module lead. How can we expect teachers to be prepared to teach a diverse range of students when the training they receive does not see this as a priority? In the following lived experience piece, SENCO Lana Crosbie will discuss what more could be done to address this in initial teacher training.

Lived experience: Lana Crosbie, associate assistant principal and SENCO

I am a Black female educator with over 20 years' experience within education. I have held many roles including teacher, head of department, associate assistant principal, coach and many more. My current role is a SENCO. Amidst all these changing roles and the deepening of my experience and understanding of effective pedagogy, the one thing that has not changed is my deeply rooted connection to my Blackness. I have been reminded of 'my place' in many nuanced ways. We now have new labels to describe these actions: microaggressions.

How many times have my White colleagues had to field these questions?

'So, where are you from?'

'Where are you really from?'

How many of them have had labels assigned to them that they did not earn or ask for?

One of my previous principals would see me in meetings or introduce me to new teachers by saying, 'Oh, here comes trouble' or 'Welcome... this is Miss Trouble.' I found myself fighting to break down a reputation that I did not ask for or earn. All of it was thinly disguised as banter or humour.

If I challenge this behaviour, I am fulfilling the stereotypical label. If I let it go, I am not using my platform to challenge racism. Amidst all of this conflict, I am a living, feeling human being, and these battle scars take their toll. But still, I rise!

As an educator, I educate the children who represent our future – the adults of tomorrow. I find myself asking the question, how can I convey what many do not understand? The lived experience is vital; it's visceral, guttural. If educators are to work with young children and adults who also have these experiences, wouldn't it make sense for the system to acknowledge the need for this to be a staple part of the training?

We would not send soldiers to war without physical and assault weapons training. We do not allow doctors to operate without many hours of practical experience. Why should the expectations for educators be any different? Why should the bar be set lower?

Rigorous teacher training should be the holy grail. It is the opportunity to understand pedagogy and andragogy before we move into our privileged positions as educators. As the gatekeepers of an educational system that purports to be inclusive and 'fit for all children', we must use our platform for good.

I would have relished the prospect during my teacher training to examine challenging concepts and ask myself questions such as: how does my positionality recognise, honour and problematise intersectional notions of difference in my practice as an educator? Sadly, it is not part of the training, even after all these years of change and reform. Currently, to gain QTS in England and Wales, you are not required to become an active advocate for anti-racist education. Therefore, we are bound to continue to perpetuate the ills of the past.

We also need to question the quest for churning out educators at a fast pace (to rectify the slump in those applying to become teachers) with quick fixes and financial incentives. What impact is this having on the lack of equity? What impact is it having on the quality of teaching and learning? With over 20 years' experience in the field, I would firmly state that we need to reform ITT programmes.

By making these changes, we can ensure we have educators who truly understand the importance of an authentic and empowering education. Educators will be able to create spaces within the curriculum to deconstruct negative stereotypes and identities, with opportunities for students and educators to learn the importance of these ideologies critically. Examples of practical methods include:

- self-portraits
- skin tone identification
- poems
- guest speakers from different cultural backgrounds.

Educators will also offer opportunities for exploration and, importantly, an examination of the links between the historical roots of oppression and the impact on all our lived experiences. This requires a skilled hand to deliver sensitively but authentically. This is not explored or taught in current ITT programmes.

We need our adults of tomorrow to understand community power and how to create change. This can be explored through the vehicle of many subjects, arming our students with the knowledge and skills to be able to enact change.

We need to move away from 'diversifying the curriculum' by including the 'usual suspects' – Martin Luther King, slavery and civil rights. These are critical points in our history, but we did not begin after slavery – slavery interrupted our history. Martin Luther King was, and is, an icon, and rightly so, but he was not alone; there were and are many others. Where is the wisdom of other significant inspiring figures? The inclusion of the other positive contributions to music, literature, history and so on. We are airbrushing out of the curriculum the parts that aren't seen as 'palatable'. How can this be considered an equitable education? We also need to examine the 'challenging topics': sexism, racism and religious intolerance, as these are also forms of oppression.

How can this be achieved in ITT programmes?

We are not arming our newly qualified teachers with the tools required to navigate multicultural classrooms successfully. They are often not equipped to address students' questions, experiences and traumas. We are equipping them to get results, get through curriculums, plan lessons – to survive as an educator. Where is the inclusion of critical race theory as a theoretical framework? Our White colleagues also need to understand and examine, for example, the impact of White Privilege. This might help to inform their positions in the classroom and staffroom and their handling of school-based issues connected to race.

A favourite quote of mine springs to mind when I think of education and how inequitable, scarring and traumatising it is for both Black, Brown and racially minoritised educators and students alike.

'Survival is not an academic skill. It is learning how to stand alone, unpopular and sometimes reviled, and how to make common cause with those others identified as outside the structures in order to define and seek a world in which we can all flourish. It is learning how to take our differences and make them strengths. The master's tools will never dismantle the master's house. They may allow us temporarily to beat him at his own game, but they will never enable us to bring about genuine change…' (Lorde, 2018)

The change needs to be a root and branch approach. The culture needs changing. At grassroots level. Not just lessons in isolation, but institutions, policies and practices. Theory alone rarely leads to a change in understanding and language. This needs to be an embedded approach that allows for repeated, safe, authentic exposure to real issues.

Lana Crosbie is an associate assistant principal, SENCO and equality, diversity and inclusion lead for a post-16 provision within a large multi-academy trust in the south-west of England.

Mentoring

In the 2020/2021 academic year, I mentored trainee teachers from the 'BIPOC' community as part of a study at Exeter University. The term BIPOC (Black, Indigenous and People of Colour) was used in the title of the programme. Part of the study sought to research the impact upon BIPOC students and their trainee journey and whether the impact of a BIPOC mentor improves their experience.

My mentees and I talked at length about our experiences. We spoke about the lack of opportunity to talk about race and anti-racist practice, despite it being so crucial to creating a culture of inclusion in the classroom. What hope can we have for new BIPOC trainees if they feel that they are excluded before they begin? The final lived experience piece in this chapter is from one of my mentees, Jivan Ward, who discusses his experiences of initial teacher training.

Lived experience: Jivan Ward, secondary English teacher

I cannot help but question the lack of representation in education, and how that has impacted my journey to becoming an English teacher. Reflecting on my experience of education was integral to my ITT as a secondary English teacher trainee, and from the beginning, it was clear that things need to improve.

Before starting secondary school, my grandmother died. I started writing poetry and short stories as a means of working through my grief. At the time, I thought important writers were English. I understood that the criteria to be accepted as 'canon' was a work's relation to Shakespeare, the Romantics and Dickens. I did not know about the rich global literature that was translated, waiting to be read.

I thought that creating essential works of fiction was a European endeavour and that the discipline was a solely European conversation. I was living in ignorance. However, I was lucky; I had a family of bookworms who illuminated the reality for me. This allowed me to read the works of writers of colour, to explore literature that was outside my experiences and knowledge, and this inspired me. Once I was aware that there were artists from other cultures contributing to the best that has ever been thought and written, I knew it was possible to be different and to be validated. In representation, I witnessed my potential.

I wish similar empowerment had inspired me to become an English teacher. If anything, my journey towards being a qualified teacher happened in spite of my experiences at secondary school and university.

After graduating, I was lucky to be able to cash in my native English speaker privilege and teach abroad. I spent a year in Catalunya and two in South Korea.

It is disingenuous to say that these experiences were entirely positive. It was life-changing, and of course good always comes with bad. Moving between countries opens up other cultures as well as all of the hang-ups and toxicity that may lie within. I believe this is true of all cultures and in all corners of the world. I learnt many things. But more than anything, living abroad demonstrated the various faces of racism, xenophobia and prejudice that manifest in different contexts.

In South Korea, my experience was different from other BAME native English teachers I met. I was light-skinned enough to be considered White; my Indo-Caribbean heritage was ignored. My West London accent and my father's hand-me-down White British facial features defined me. This was in direct contrast to my experience in the UK. After Brexit and the Windrush Scandal, I felt a tangible difference. What I thought were fundamental British values were no more than rhetoric. In Britain, I did not feel British; in South Korea, I was nothing but. This experience triggered a confrontation within me. I was faced with the fractured duality of culture and history that manifested in my mixed-raced existence. One that is largely ignored in British culture and education.

This awakening was not singular. It was while teaching abroad that I realised I had something to offer and teach. Otherwise, I had no plans to be a teacher. Every English teacher I had throughout my education was White British. I never had a BAME/BIPOC English teacher. My experience correlates with a study conducted by UCL Institute of Education published in 2020. It found that nearly half of UK schools have no BAME teachers, and that most BAME teachers are located in London. Although I grew up in London, I only had four BAME teachers throughout my entire education. This lack of representation stopped me from seeing my potential to be a teacher.

Early into my ITT, I realised that English literature is defined by its nationalistic determiner. There is no 'English' music or drama. There is no Scottish or Welsh or Irish literature studied at GCSE in England. This is furthered by a cognitive dissonance. At Key Stage 3, teachers can teach the books that they want (school and English department curriculum permitting). This is an opportunity to teach diverse books, but this is predicated on the teacher's tastes and knowledge of diverse and global literature. English language and literature education are mainly mono-cultural and mono-linguistic throughout the entire primary to undergraduate cycle.

In my ITT, I had to read a selection of books on GCSE exam boards. The only diverse books by BAME/BIPOC authors were *Anita and Me* and *Never Let Me Go*. There is no mandatory opportunity for teacher trainees to improve their knowledge of diverse British and global texts. This is a wasted opportunity to educate trainees in diverse literature.

It is worth noting that the publishing industry does not help much either. A survey conducted by the Centre for Literacy in Primary Education called

'Reflecting realities' (2021) concluded that out of 5,875 UK children's books published in 2020 only 879 featured characters of colour, and only eight per cent of them had an ethnic minority main protagonist. Just four years previously, in 2017, this figure was even more shocking at only one per cent.

Perhaps the most confusing aspect of my ITT is that throughout the course, my instructors were conscious of the need for diversity and inclusivity in education. Still, every safeguarding lecture and seminar I attended never raised racism as an issue, as if it was not an issue that could affect a student's wellbeing. This is an oversight.

Trainees are taught to spot signs of Islamic fundamentalism in Prevent training but are not trained how to spot signs of racial abuse in schools. Anti-racism was a whiff in the wind, only to be undertaken by trainees who cared enough to seek out the information and educate themselves. As the only BAME male student in my ITT cohort, this was isolating.

At the heart of literature is a fundamental search for truth, as experienced. It is at its most potent when it questions, when it illuminates and when it represents the moral and philosophical dichotomies within us and the transcendence of living in and sharing in stories. Stories are universal, and they are a straightforward way to learn about other people, whilst learning about ourselves. This is the power and promise of literature education.

There is no discernible reason for English literature to be mainly monocultural.

I believe education is most powerful in open communication with students, in navigation between knowledge to be learnt, knowledge that is understood, and knowledge that has already been experienced. Education is meant to aid and empower students in understanding and navigating the world they were born into. Every student deserves to learn about the world in all of its multicultured glory. If nothing changes, we will foster another generation ignorant to the complexities of racism, and the empowerment of diversity. We will fail if future generations cannot see their full potential.

Jivan Ward is an educator and writer. He was part of a mentoring scheme at Exeter University where he was mentored by Aisha.

Question

Why is English literature so nationalistic and insular? Why are the diasporic literatures of millions of British citizens ignored in education?

We have an expectation that all teachers are ready to teach all children (see the Swann Report, 'Education for all', 1985). Yet, we only provide Eurocentric educational preparation. It is therefore not surprising that so many teachers and educators feel ill prepared for conversations around race. It is not uncommon to hear 'X has been racist to Y – what should we do?' It is as if the words race and racism force many people into a ball of fear, uncertainty, denial and disregard – and educators do not feel prepared for the next steps. Teacher training needs to tackle this head-on but this can't be done in a one-off, tick-box CPD session. We need to be preparing educators to teach children of all backgrounds, and this starts with initial teacher training and continues with mentoring, reflective practice and ongoing CPD.

Summary

Key learning points

- Training on anti-racist practices cannot simply take the form of an annual e-module or INSET day. It must be embedded throughout ITT programmes and form part of a teacher's ongoing reflective practice and CPD.
- Consider the Teachers' Standards through the lens of race: to achieve their QTS, are teachers meeting the needs of all children to the highest standard, irrespective of cultural heritage or background?
- ITT programmes must commit to preparing teachers for multicultural classrooms. Trainees need to be equipped to address students' questions, experiences and trauma, examine the impact of White Privilege and handle school-based issues connected to race. To achieve this, training providers must change their culture, policies and practices.
- The Early Career Framework (Department for Education, 2021e) has a renewed emphasis on mentoring for early career teachers. However, there is no explicit reference to anti-racist practice. As the British population becomes more racially diverse and multicultural, it is important that teachers have an opportunity to gain this knowledge and challenge their thinking through mentoring.

Key question

Did you have anti-racist CPD during your teacher training?

a) Yes, I feel adequately prepared.

b) Yes, but there is so much more to learn.

c) Some, but I still do not feel comfortable.

d) None, I don't know where to begin.

Further self-reflection questions

1. Why is anti-racism not a part of ITT?
2. Why aren't teachers taught to question their bias and their prejudicial and stereotypical views?
3. How many students are dissuaded from becoming a teacher because they are not represented by the teaching population?
4. Why have those who have held the posts of Chief Inspector of Schools, Secretary of State for Education and school's minister all rejected the calls for change in the education system (Weale, 2020; Duffy, 2020; Merrick, 2021)?

Discussion points for staff meetings

- We want to ensure that all teachers and educators are racially literate and truly inclusive. Yet there is no mandatory requirement for anti-racist practice training or bias training during the teacher training programme. If we truly want to move forward and ensure that teacher training practice is inclusive, what steps do we need to take to make it happen?

- Do you feel the responsibility of supporting Black, Brown and racially minoritised children often falls to the Person of Colour in your setting? Who would usually be responsible for behavioural needs related to the children of colour in your school? Do you believe all teachers are adequately prepared to support and understand the Black, Brown and racially minoritised children in their school?

9 Inclusive practice

'Accessibility is being able to get into the building.
Diversity is getting invited to the table.
Inclusion is having a voice at the table.
Belonging is having your voice heard.
Justice is choosing if you want to be there in the first place.'

Source unknown

Meetings can be a microcosm of a school's culture and how individuals behave within it. Meetings may reveal what is important, who is valued and what are the school values. Examining your next staff meeting is a helpful starting point for analysing inclusive practice in your school. What is happening in the meeting may reflect what is happening between teachers and students in classrooms, in corridors and on the school playground. As educators, it is important for us to be aware of the threat of erasure and the dominant voices we continue to hear that silence the voices of others.

Training on equality, diversity and inclusion can often be a starting point on this journey, but as we discovered in Chapter 8, it is often treated as an annual tick-box exercise and does not provide the opportunity for staff to explore their own identity and understanding of the world. As bell hooks says, educators must embed self-actualisation and self-reflection as part of a process of continuous personal and professional development, and this is absolutely critical when it comes to ensuring inclusive practice.

Activity

As educators, we can spend a lot of time in meetings. As an assistant principal, I probably spent 50 per cent of my week in meetings. But when I reflect on my time in the senior leadership meeting room, I wonder: was my voice heard? Who held the room? Who was included?

The next time you are in a meeting, observe who holds the space. Whose voice is being heard? Who is getting across their ideas? Note down your observations.

> Then, at the next meeting, agree that everyone will have an opportunity to speak. Perhaps take it in turns and set a time limit, for example, one minute per person. To ensure this is meaningful, you may split tasks on the agenda or ask everyone for an update on the work that they are doing.
>
> The impact of this activity, I hope, is inclusion.

Facilitating an inclusive environment

In the following lived experience piece, Ronnie Kisubi, a diversity and equality lead, provides some practical advice for facilitating an inclusive environment in your school.

Lived experience: Ronnie Kisubi, geography teacher and head of diversity and inclusion

In my teaching career, I have never been offered training on diversity, inclusion or anti-racism. Perhaps, in the past, I didn't look hard enough for it, but it certainly was never offered. Formal training around inclusivity is available, but if it isn't on your radar, you will not find it. There are many avenues for training. It entirely depends on your educational setting's needs, whether that be staff training, resources for lessons, PSHE needs or curriculum needs. The Black Curriculum is a great starting place, offering insightful resources through their website and social media and offering in-house training for schools on inclusivity and decolonising the curriculum.

My household is multiracial; my children are mixed race, so making sure that I know how to educate my children around their race, culture and how others in the world around them may see them has always been at the forefront of my mind. I try to ensure I bring this practice to school with me every day because the Black and ethnic minority students who are in front of me, well, they are someone else's children and these parents and carers are also working hard at home to nurture them and empower them. Is it not our job to support this too? However, why should it only be the people who have a personal investment in inclusion and race, whether that be their own race or the race of their family and children, who are the ones to drive inclusivity and anti-racism in schools forward? Should it not be on every educator's mind to be more inclusive and anti-racist in their everyday practice?

If the students are always the priority, then the desire to be more inclusive should be a priority for everyone. As has been established in Chapter 2, diversity is the 'what' and inclusion is the 'how', and unfortunately you can have diversity without an inclusive culture. Inclusion is a cultural measure that allows a diverse community to thrive. Facilitating an inclusive environment within your educational setting benefits all school community members and not just the members who want to feel included. White students will broaden their understanding of different races, cultures and languages, whilst instead of perhaps just tolerating others who are different to themselves, they will embrace them and empathetically understand the struggles that others may have. For Black and ethnic minority students, an inclusive environment allows them to thrive, to see themselves within their day-to-day education, to feel represented. It provides them with role models to look up to, people they aspire to be like and a feeling of more equal opportunities within their education. For educators, it can open their eyes to the experiences of their Black and ethnic minority students.

I have heard many teachers say, 'But I have always treated everyone the same.' There has been a limited understanding that this thought process has not created an equal environment. By broadening the inclusive environment, it comes to understanding that equity must come before equality to allow a more level playing field. This cannot be done by simply treating everyone the same. This needs to be done by raising the most disadvantaged students' profiles and allowing them access to the same opportunities. Without acknowledging the disproportionate barriers that many Black and ethnic minority students face in both their personal lives and their education setting, equality can never truly be enjoyed. Racial equity should be imagined a bit like a five-foot brick wall with something exciting happening on the other side (like a sports match). Imagine that three people are behind the wall; one is six foot tall, one is five foot tall, and the other is four foot tall. If you gave each person a one-foot-tall box to stand on, the six-foot-tall person, who already had a good view over the wall, now has an even better view. The five-foot-tall person now also has a good view; however, the four-foot-tall person can still not see over the wall. This would be classed as equality; everyone has been given the same thing. However, to provide equity, the six-foot person does not need a box at all, the five-foot person needs one box and the four-foot person needs two boxes. This way, all three people are standing at the height of six foot to see over the wall. No additional boxes were required, but merely a reshuffle based on each individual's barriers, thus providing equity, where equality can be enjoyed, together.

As an educator, there is often the expectation that we can teach anything, particularly when it comes to PSHE. This can be from finances to mental health, sex education to bullying, cultural holidays to politics around the world. The list is endless and teachers provide this learning experience day in and day out. But, when it comes to lessons about race, racial bullying or anti-racism, they either don't exist within that school environment or teachers can shy away from the subject and feel unsure how to deliver them. Instead of this being a reflection on the individual who may be uncomfortable, this should highlight a broader need to boost the staff's confidence in delivering the content to ensure that they do it justice for the students in front of them. I have witnessed sessions where the teacher did not feel comfortable or confident with the content they had to deliver and this led to the students receiving a basic and stripped-back version of the content, with little discussion time for questions to arise and not much of an opportunity to break down any barriers. This can create what can be interpreted by students as a box-ticking exercise and highlight the lack of care or passion for the topic at hand. Often this can be more detrimental than not delivering the content at all. To facilitate the most productive PSHE environment, where staff feel confident to deliver inclusive content and students feel empowered with opportunities to ask questions, resources must be broken down to staff with clear instructions and training with an open-forum format, to allow everyone to ask questions and feel supported in doing so. This should result in each adult delivering the sessions in the most effective way, promoting healthy discussion between adult and students.

Ronnie Kisubi is a geography teacher and head of diversity and inclusion who is making a secondary school in South East England a more inclusive place through elevating the experiences of its Black students and students of colour, teacher training, and diversifying the curriculum.

Question

How often are you receiving training to support you in delivering lesson content about race and anti-racist practices?

a) It is embedded in all we do and forms part of an ongoing and regular CPD programme.

b) Once per term.

c) Once per year.

d) On an ad hoc basis, for example to teach a specific lesson or module.

e) When it is topical.

f) I can't remember.

The consequences of not having an inclusive school environment

Listening to the experiences of adults as they reflect on their childhood, it has become even more apparent to me that schools need to adapt their inclusive practice to ensure they are supporting the children and young people they are serving. Every educator must take responsibility for creating a more inclusive environment in classrooms, corridors, playgrounds, staffrooms, meeting rooms and offices, and must make a commitment to equity, not just equality. In order to achieve this, educators need adequate training.

If this work is not done, schools run the risk of perpetuating the cycle of racial trauma. Often Black, Brown and racially minoritised people are carrying trauma with them for years and it is impacting on how they engage and also how their descendants engage after them. It is as if the baton of trauma is continually being handed down from generation to generation. As we will see in the next lived experience piece, what happens to a young Black, Brown or racially minoritised person in a school setting can remain with them for the rest of their lives. My great-grandmother and my grandmother both experienced the years of 'No cats, no dogs, no Blacks and no Irish'. Their children lived through the showing of *Roots* and images of Africans with flies on their noses and living in mud huts. And if this is what is happening to those with lived experience of racial trauma in their educational career, what is happening to White children and young people? What are their ancestors passing down?

Training needs to be provided to combat this narrative and provide a sense of inclusion throughout a school setting. It can't simply be a case of cultural fit! How often are Black, Brown and racially minoritised people drawn upon to be the source of knowledge? To be the person who makes the environment safe? To be the person who draws upon all of their knowledge and wisdom to act as living CPD? But what about this person's own racial trauma? Constantly being the go-to person expected to take charge of incidents of racism, discussions about race and anti-racist practices just because of the colour of your skin can be both exhausting and triggering. Schools must not rely on Black, Brown and racially minoritised educators to do this work. All educators regardless of background need to be empowered to take responsibility for this work every moment of every day.

If we are products of our environment, we need to ask ourselves what contribution we are making to the communal environment right now. Whose responsibility is it to create hospitable conditions for us all to learn, grow and develop? And this is especially important when considering our children. Academic institutions play a significant role in this process.

I can vividly remember a lesson on slavery, the one where the slave ship image gets presented. Slaves packed into the bowls of ships like sardines. Little black stick-like characters in horizontal rows upon rows upon rows. It gave me an overwhelming surge of rage. Surprising? Not really! I'm dual heritage. I saw myself reflected back. I saw my father, my aunts, my cousins, my kin, the community. The anger this image stirred manifested physically and I kicked the table leg.

I was summoned to the front of the class, being the only young person of 'colour' in the room; I looked around to see how other students were responding. With their heads slightly buried in what I can only imagine now was immense discomfort. Coupled with an active attempt to avoid eye contact with me, they were doing OK in comparison. I made my way up to the front of the classroom.

I was asked to explain what the problem was. As if it wasn't obvious why this young person, just a teenager, with hormones surging, personality still forming, physically and emotionally still under construction, would kick the table leg. 'Contain yourself' was the sub-context. 'Get this display of emotion under control immediately' was the unspoken message.

I couldn't express myself then like I would now on this subject matter. I didn't have the vocabulary, skills or tools to say, 'This feels fucked up!' To say, 'Teachers shouldn't be teaching the subject of transatlantic slavery while lacking the essential facilitation skills to manage the emotions that are certain to come up as a result of such a history lesson.' I often think about how these emotions manifest for different personality types. I think myself lucky that I was raised to acknowledge and express such feelings. I was sent back to my seat and told to control myself.

25 years later I find myself writing about this moment. A moment in time that will forever remain imprinted on my mind. It showed me that not all responsible adults in my life were willing to take responsibility. Certainly a sign of the times, however; one would hope now that teachers have the insight and compassion needed in these lessons. To take us through this time of transformation, it's estimated that by 2050 a quarter of the British population will be considered Black, Asian and Minoritised Ethnic. How we tell our story to the next generation requires vulnerability, honesty and authenticity.

Katie Donovan-Adekanmbi *is an inclusion and cohesion specialist, and founder of BCohCo Ltd (Building Cohesive Communities). Through their work, BCohCo supports organisations to create conditions for genuine cultural change.*

Lived experience: Malcolm Richards, educator

It is through my entry, socialisation and successful navigations within the formal educational system that I have in part, I would argue, benefited from luck, privilege and access which has been rarely afforded to people who look, sound or act like me. While there are benefits – my experiences as student, teacher and now academic, statistically, morally, and professionally – the cost is high. Like many educational professionals, I asked myself and others the question – why do we continue to do this? In this brief outline, I offer three reflections on experiences of my past which seek to answer this question.

Between the ages of eight and 13 years old, I attended two African/Caribbean supplementary schools in the London Borough of Hackney: Josina Machel Supplementary School (Clapton) and Dimbaleh Education Centre (Dalston). It was there that I engaged with a group of **community elders** who were able to open knowledge, understandings and connections with ancestral and cultural 'practices' from across the African diaspora. As members of our extended families, our community elders were truly intercultural, representative of Gilroy's Black Atlantic (1993). All were skilled, whether in storytelling, practical and technical engineering, growing or spiritual matters, though not conventionally trained teachers. Their 'universal' connection was the ability to create teaching and learning spaces where valuing of our diverse community's histories, traditions, and repertoires took place. I still reflect upon how these experiences were given equal understanding, positioned as legitimate, mystical, and intergenerational ways of life.

These are ways of 'teaching' that I have very rarely seen in schooling, yet whose outcomes and evaluations continue to astound. It was clear that these ways of eldership should be treasured, with time taken to make meaning and understanding of what it means to embark on a journey towards (re)claiming our cultural practices. The first time I saw this sense of community eldership replicated in my formal schooling experience was when **Mr O.G.** walked into our design and technology classroom at the beginning of Year 8. Six foot three. Broad shoulders. The look of someone who was at home. He introduced himself with a deep baritone voice, explaining that he would be our teacher for design and technology. We stood at the workbenches open mouthed. I'm not sure who, but one of my peers asked him where he was from. We knew he was 'small island', Nevis or Montserrat. Just in that opening phrasing, we knew – and he knew – that he spoke to us like we spoke to each other. It was the most wonderful, affirming thing. It is only now that I realise how fortunate I was to be surrounded by community elders, or teachers, who literally looked like me, spoke like me, and had the same cultural references as me. Mr O.G. understood the importance of his place and space in that classroom for us. He valued all our traditions and ways of being. He saw us, he understood us. He was us.

It is rare to see a teacher with dreadlocks, moreover a teacher who is Rastafarl. As my experiences indicate, I have been blessed and highly favoured to meet a few. One fleeting meeting continues to resonate. It took place in my first teaching post, early in my career, as I was walking quickly along a corridor towards a cover lesson. Stressed. In the opposite direction, a Rastafarl teacher was calmly walking in the opposite direction. Our eyes locked, we smiled, and offered a universal salutation. I felt instant calm. Serenity. The opposite of the dominant normative projections of teachers with dreadlocks, and by extension Rastafarl. An expectation which demands the wearer to be critical, to be rebellious, to in some way explore ways of knowing outside of the norms and values of what we collectively expect. I saw this wonderful Rastafarl teacher a few times afterwards, exchanged brief words and greetings and offered a salutation. I soon left the school, moving onto new and exciting things. I've not since seen him. But I've never forgotten him. I've never forgotten the serenity, the calmness, the sense of 'peace'.

In 2017, when I began my trod towards Rastafarl, I knew that part of my acknowledging a new way of life was to grow dreadlocks, in recognition of a spiritual, political, cultural and historical experience that I have always been connected to. This overstanding was, I think, reinforced when I was a boy, and so it remains now. Many elements have contributed to this journey, including the experiences I have shared. It could have been my dad's love of Roots Reggae, the wonder experienced whenever hearing Aisha speak. I also place much emphasis on the reasonings with my brother Imran, talking about education, Rastafarl and Islam as ways of life. By my shifting, changing yet very visible act of representation, especially in the southwest of England, I know that my (meta)physical being stands for something more than just my own expression of consciousness. Whether in classrooms, speaker series or higher education institution tutorials, I represent a minority and minoritised community, who is a statistical anomaly within the educational space. I also must acknowledge that I continue to be part of structures which value pedagogical practices, and adhere to legislation, policies and professional cultures which erase ways of being and knowing. If our students, families and communities continue to evaluate my words and work as valuable and allow me to continue to be part of their educational experiences, perhaps they remain happy that we continue to build relationships towards educational transformations.

Why do I continue to do this? In the spaces and places that I inhabit, as one of one, perhaps our students, families, peers and communities haven't truly *seen* us here before.

My representation matters.

Malcolm Richards is an educator, scholar-activist, independent doctoral researcher, and co-founder of Bookbag, an independent bookshop based in Exeter, Devon (UK).

Summary

Key learning points

- We must do the work to empower ourselves and gain knowledge so we feel confident to take individual responsibility for facilitating an inclusive school environment.
- Educational establishments must invest in adequate and regular CPD for their staff to support them in inclusive practice.
- Safe spaces should be created for courageous and uncomfortable conversations.
- We must see the distinction between diversity and inclusion training and anti-racist practice training. The former is a palatable version of change. The latter requires us to deconstruct and dismantle our thinking and the very systems that we serve.

Key question

How important is anti-racist practice?

a) I think it should be mandatory.
b) I think it should apply to schools where it affects the demographic.
c) I think it should be discussed when relevant.
d) I think it is too political. It does not have a place in school.

Inclusive practice

Further self-reflection questions

1. What do you mean when you use the word 'inclusive'? What lens are you looking through when you discuss your classroom or school as an 'inclusive environment'?
2. Do you feel you have adequate knowledge and training to be a part of creating an inclusive environment in your school?
3. If so, is inclusivity something you consider and prioritise in every part of your teaching practice?
4. If not, where are your knowledge gaps and what steps could you take to fill them? What is holding you back?

Discussion points for staff meetings

- Consider if the focus needs to be on training educators or improving provisions for students in order to facilitate inclusive practice in your setting.
- What are the initial training needs of the staff within your education setting?
- Where are the opportunities in your setting to provide more equity?
- How will you facilitate a proactive and inclusive environment? Create a short-term and medium-term plan and consider how you can create a more sustainable ethos and embed a culture of inclusivity.

10 Challenging my racism

'Your silence will not protect you.'

Audre Lorde (2017)

How do you challenge racism?

How do you approach racial incidents?

What threshold does an incident need to meet in order for it to be challenged?

Who decides that threshold?

I have experienced many examples of racism in my life. Some overt, some covert. But the interesting fact for me is that in most cases there was always an audience or a witness. Even in the presence of others, the struggle to report my experience of racism was commonplace, to the extent that I no longer wanted to challenge it. What was the point? It seemed to be 'acceptable' racism that most had come to terms with as the norm.

I remember collecting my son from a school trip when he was in primary school. He was the only Black child and I was collecting him from a pick-up point in an area of Bristol which is well known for racism. I attended with my younger son and my niece. As I got out of the car, within a few moments, a man walking his dog and accompanied by his young child started hurling abuse at me. This abuse included various disturbing racial slurs. I told the kids to get back in the car. There were several parents present who were also collecting their children. Yet not one parent offered support or challenged the man for how he was talking to me. I often wonder if there were any circumstances in which support would have been offered to me. If the comments were gendered, would things have been different? I guess I will never know.

My question to you is this: how often do you step in and challenge racism when you are witnessing it? Are there circumstances when you wouldn't do this? Would you feel comfortable challenging a child who was being racist towards another child? What about if it was an adult being racist to a child?

We deal with incidents of racism in different ways depending on who's involved. Often it's relatively simple to deal with an incident between two children: we step in and use behaviour management techniques and our school's behaviour policy to challenge the child involved. Challenging another staff member is much harder. Our response to the situation and the urgency with which we deal with it changes radically depending on who the perpetrator is.

The law states that the victim, or any other individual, only needs to perceive that a criminal offence is racist or motivated by religious hate for it to be classified as a hate crime. This means that if *you* believe an incident is a hate incident, it should be recorded as such. Yet it is rarely that simple. In fact, most often racism is denied. Phrases such as 'That was not my intention', 'My Black friend said it was OK', 'Oh, but I heard it in a music video', 'It was a joke', 'Slavery was years ago' and 'I don't see colour' are often rebuttals that are received.

Yet we know that racism can cause deep-rooted trauma and, if not challenged, in the worst cases can result in deep-rooted hatred and death.

Overt and covert racism

When we think of racism, we often think of acts of bigotry that are explicit and 'visible'. From racist insults to racial insensitivities and microaggressions, these 'overt' forms of racism present themselves in schools on a regular basis and we need to know how to deal with them. However, overt racism is just the tip of the iceberg. Beneath the surface lies a whole host of other forms of racism, which may be implicit and 'invisible', but are equally as damaging. This 'covert' racism is deeply embedded in the British education system and therefore in our everyday practices in school, and it can be much harder to tackle.

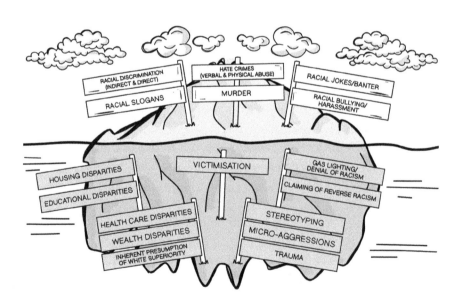

Dealing with overt incidents of racism

When dealing with an incident of overt racism, educators often try to grapple with how severe it is. I have heard comments such as 'Oh but it was casual racism' or 'It was low level; it wasn't the N-word' or 'I have heard worse!'. As long as we are categorising racism and tiering it on a scale of severity in this way, we are ignoring the most important point: a child, young person or peer has been subject to racial abuse. That has an impact on them and it constitutes a form of hatred based on the colour of their skin. There shouldn't be a debate as to whether it has met a fictional threshold based on personal experience and bias. If racism has taken place, it should be acknowledged as a safeguarding concern and recorded as such.

The victim should be at the centre, and centring their needs should come before what sometimes feels like a race to punish the other party or parties and shut the situation down. The emphasis is on the rule or policy that has been broken, rather than the values and culture of the school that have been impacted. The result is usually a detention or a period of isolation. Does this constitute taking racism seriously?

Education for the perpetrator is extremely important. Their parents and carers must be informed. It's also important to give them an opportunity to rebuild the relationship and understand why racism is wrong. However, superficial handshakes and apologies such as 'I am sorry if you felt it was racist' are problematic and demonstrate that the issue or racism in this incident has been inadequately understood by the person who is responsible. Time should be spent to investigate and respond with true care and attention. Check trends and records. Is there data to show that there is a pattern of this kind of behaviour? Is it related to recent events? Is there a need for curriculum input, assemblies or a tutor programme to address the circumstances related to the incident?

The reality is that racism is everywhere. We cannot always clearly separate it out. It sometimes takes time and attention to detect and decipher what has happened. An intersectional lens is needed as it is often that the abuse may be coupled with another form of oppression. It is deeply embedded in our structures and is often subject to perception, experiences and bias. A form of racism to be aware of is anti-Blackness: behaviours, attitudes and practices of individuals and institutions that work to dehumanise Black people (see page 203). As discussed in previous chapters, the ways in which one identifies with themselves and others and the way they view the world will impact how they interact and respond.

Many educators will strive for a zero-tolerance approach. But what does a zero-tolerance approach to racism mean? It can sometimes be interpreted as 'no discussion', which in turn leads to an erasure of opportunity to understand what has happened and the impact upon the victim. Racism is abhorrent and can never be justified, but a poorly managed zero-tolerance approach will shut down the opportunity for education.

A restorative framework for dealing with overt incidents of racism

There needs to be a clear understanding of what racism is, and the entire school community need to hold a collective responsibility. Restorative justice can be an effective way for a school to demonstrate a collective approach to tackling racism. Peer-led leadership amongst pupils, mediation, PSHE and curriculum input are all great avenues to challenge unwanted behaviour in school. A good restorative model will allow humanity to be centralised. There should be a clear process and outcome, conducted by an impartial third party who will ensure safety, clear communication and integrity throughout the process. It should allow space for understanding, discomfort and accountability. There is no focus on a winner or loser, but instead on the ability to be heard, seen and included.

Step 1: Acknowledge what has taken place.
Step 2: Ensure that the victim is supported and is safe.
Step 3: Help the perpetrator to understand the victim's experience and how it has impacted them.
Step 4: Inform parents and carers.
Step 5: Share the learning with the class or other staff members.

Challenging covert racism

It is far easier to see overt racism and often for us to challenge it through our existing behaviour policies and procedures. However, what can be more difficult is the covert racism, the insidious racism. The 'I do not see colour' kind of racism. This is likely present in our everyday classroom practices, in what we're teaching and how we're teaching it, and in our interactions with pupils, parents and colleagues – and we might not even be aware of it.

When considering experiences of covert racism, it is important that the voices of those for whom it is a lived experience are heard. Teachers and schools must then take action to implement change that is not only seen but also felt. If you're a teacher, listen to the experiences of the pupils in your class, think about what you could do differently in your classroom in light of what they are saying and implement those changes promptly but carefully. Remember the need to challenge racism is not simply for Black, Brown and racially minoritised children.

White children need to understand the history and see the problematic nature of what has been taught in the past. If you're a school leader, try conducting a pupil survey or a pupil voice session to listen to experiences and viewpoints across the school. Canvas school staff for their stories and opinions too, either in a staff survey or a staff meeting. Think about what can be done at a more strategic level to implement change across your department or setting to benefit all stakeholders.

Working through reflective activities regarding racial identity and racism as a whole-school community may also be a useful way to provoke discussion and ascertain a way forward. The following activity provides a starting point for reflection as an individual, as a staff body and with a class of pupils.

Activity

Personal reflection

Take a moment to reflect on the following in relation to you as an individual:

- Think about your relationship with race and racism.
- When did you first realise that you were deemed to be of a particular race?
- What was the experience?

Staff reflection

In your next team meeting, provide a safe space for staff to discuss their relationship with race and privilege, and challenge them to question the experiences they have had both personally and professionally.

Pupil reflection

Provide pupils with the opportunity for the exploration of identity. Ask them to think about who they are, what they look like and where they live.

Then get them to consider their classmates and the adults around them. Ask them to explore the differences that exist and provide the opportunity to celebrate the amazing uniqueness that they all bring.

Lived experience: Rodeane Henry-Grant, educator, linguist and ludologist

Formal education prepares young people for life and employment outside of school. Therefore, schools must focus on anti-racism work to avoid the reproduction of racist norms in society.

The reasons why this work isn't yet happening are many. Teachers lack the confidence and expertise to effectively teach pre-colonial history. This can lead to inferiorisation, embarrassment and disengagement from Black, Brown and racially minoritised pupils. There is also an element of defensiveness when a Black, Brown or racially minoritised pupil challenges history. Many teachers welcome working with experts in this field. However, they can be blocked by decisions made by the school board regarding who can get access to the school. This may also be impacted by academy status, which means the local authority has less influence. Anti-racism must be consistently applied.

Recently I was told about how a school in the Midlands hired a new organisation to do anti-racist work with them. It was White-led. This person then proceeded to tell the staff that White people also experience racism, like being called a 'milky bar'. In my last comprehensive school, it was mandatory to attend CPD on how to deal with racism at school. This training was also White-led. The school only had three members of staff from the Global Majority at the time. My gut feeling told me that we were all experiencing the same torment.

This same school had a Year 10 student who called me the 'N-word'. They were 'fixed-term excluded', only to return and verbally abuse me again. I had a banana skin thrown at me through a window but was told that there were 'no racist intentions' by a White cis male who was the safeguarding lead and a White cis female 'mentor' who ridiculed my colleagues' accents and called me aggressive when using the 'teacher look', a favourite trope used to silence members of the Global Majority.

Intersectional invisibility is what causes the Global Majority to keep their cool when confronted with daily violence and other microaggressions to keep their jobs, or how justified anger is deemed an unprofessional or inappropriate response. This everyday racism is having a profound effect on our health, both physically and mentally.

Rodeane Henry-Grant is an educator, linguist, ludologist, and a co-founder of the Coalition of Anti-Racist Educators, a grassroots network committed to the eradication of racism within the education sector. https://nomoreexclusions.com/care/ Twitter: @CARE2Liberate

What does true solidarity against racism look like?

When it comes to challenging racism, Dr Muna Abdi makes a distinction between 'allyship' and 'solidarity'. She argues that 'The conversation can no longer be about standing beside those impacted by oppressive systems, but by working with them to effect change. It's time to move beyond allyship and into a space of solidarity.'

Dr Abdi explained to me that 'allyship enables those who self-identify as allies to engage with anti-oppressive work on their own terms, allowing them to maintain their place within the structures or systems with minimal loss or risk. Allyship constructs a distance and a seemingly concrete binary experience between people. Solidarity, on the other hand, recognises that we are interdependent and the work we must do requires deep introspection, sacrifice, and a commitment to protecting each other's dignity. Solidarity is a humanising effort, whereas performed allyship reconstructs the same dehumanising effects of the systems we live and work within.' For Dr Abdi, true solidarity is:

- Not just about being a supporter; it's about acknowledging that we all have a stake in the fight against racism.
- Relinquishing power and working through tensions and conflict, even at the risk of personal loss.
- Taking personal responsibility: ensuring that marginalised groups don't have to carry the burden of educating you, sharing their narratives of trauma and holding you to account. (Abdi, 2021)

In this next lived experience piece, Katie Friedman will discuss what solidarity means to her as a teacher, leader and coach.

Lived experience: Katie Friedman, leadership coach and neurodiversity trainer

Anti-racism is a manifestation of what it is to be human, to constantly question the layers of poisoned messaging we have imbibed since birth. By relentlessly looking at the forces which dehumanise us, our wellbeing feels more secure. When we are safe and well, we can be who we really are, not who we pretend to be or are scared of being (Ditzler, 2006). If we could ensure the psychological safety of the whole school community, imagine how incredible education could be.

My parents were often agitators trying to effect change from the outside of institutions, so as an educator I wanted to do things differently and change things from within. I witnessed endemic racism in my teenage years in the low expectations teachers had of my Black, Brown and White working-class mates in my predominantly middle-class comprehensive school. Many, especially boys, were permanently excluded before the five years were out; I went into education to do better.

What hindered me was that I did not know who I was or what part my White Privilege played in teaching and leadership. Urban diverse schools were often described as 'challenging', which I think was code for 'difficult behaviour that I don't understand and feel more comfortable judging'. On reflection, what really makes urban diverse schools 'challenging' is that they are predominantly run by benevolent White leaders who have not done the work on understanding their Whiteness and can't hold the space for those they serve who often don't hold White Privilege. These leaders are accountable to government systems that replicate and perpetuate neoliberalism, which underpins structural racism.

To drive up standards, the government leans on one of the only tools left in a shrunken state, placing huge emphasis on education to fix the mess of inequality and its own austerity-driven policies. These expectations are issued without funding or careful thinking of how to avoid replicating precisely what needs to change. This pressure causes task-driven leaders, overwhelmed with initiatives, to plug gaps like unsustainable superheroes. Busyness and fear become fertile ground for White apathy and simplistic, tokenistic solutions to what then gets lazily referred to as the diversity 'issue'. Leaders need time and space to think through long-term structural change but need and must ensure that when they do there is cognitive diversity ('difference in perspectives and thinking styles'; Syed, 2019) in the room.

Anti-racist work for White people therefore is about knowing your shit rather than knowing you're shit.

The shame and fear of the latter gives way to all kinds of defensive games: White fragility; perfectionism and fear of getting it wrong; White saviourism and White exceptionalism (Saad, 2020). Leaders need to understand who they are and how they fit into and benefit from patriarchal White structures. This means dismantling the idea of a meritocracy and being open and honest about accrued privilege. Here is my example:

> I am a White, British, university-educated, cisgender, straight woman who jointly owns her own property. I am not judged by the colour of my skin before I open my mouth to speak. I can travel to the countryside and all parts

of the city and feel that I will not be abused, attacked or mistreated for the way my skin tone has been racialised. My Whiteness is represented in history, adverts, films and books from a place of power and agency. As a parent, I don't have to prepare my boys for an unfair system set up to discount and exclude them. When teachers call me about conflict in their school or I experience conflict in my work, I do not have to spend time considering if this has racial undertones and whether I have the bandwidth or language to manage it.

When I became an educational leader, however, game-playing in the system got in the way of changing the system. I remember a conversation with a White woman who commented that schools' obsession with uniform replicated suits worn by White men, encouraging assimilation rather than system change. My instinct was that this colleague was misguided and that waiting for system change during children's short time in education would end up being a White social experiment where Black, Brown and racially minoritised children were disadvantaged further. My approach was to equip children to be able to take a seat at the table of power with their White counterparts in private schools, with strong literacy skills and high standards, including wearing blazers and learning the handshakes of privilege.

I realise that my approach meant expecting Black, Brown and racially minoritised people to ultimately change the system in the long term. Looking back, we needed a safe place to discuss privilege in order to then confidently hold space for children in their school and their developing identities. We needed a curriculum which supported this and celebrated a range of narratives, cultures and communities. Here are a few of the successes, failures and key learnings I have experienced in this endeavour.

As a teacher

As a Spanish teacher, I had been privileged to spend time in Latin America and was able to bring a range of cultural knowledge, above and beyond a European angle, to my teaching. However, when I first joined the school, I could not fully appreciate the achievements of the established community languages team. I did not immediately recognise that conserving cultural heritage and identity through the learning of their community languages was important to people living in White supremacy. Thankfully, I had a head of community languages who spent time and energy educating me and calling me in, alongside his day job. We then went on to collaborate and together ran amazing community events where staff and parents cooked the food of their heritage and taught the basics of language to all of our students. Joy and humanity were celebrated.

As a leader

Whilst we were a great community school, we were woefully underachieving. The benevolent majority White leaders were grateful to the majority White teaching staff who dedicated themselves to working in a 'challenging' school. Many in the leadership team liked to continually quote the deprivation statistics and 'mothered' or 'rescued' the children. This approach was facilitated by the liberal politics of the time where 'value added' helped to acknowledge context but links between expectations of staff and attainment of the children they served were not addressed.

Talk about racism or anti-racism was non-existent. As a middle leader, I remember challenging the fact that a Black child in care had been excluded for hitting another middle leader whose teaching was inadequate and who was known to be provocative with children. This vulnerable child was paying with his education because teachers were rarely challenged for their practice and the power dynamics of White Privilege were not openly discussed. I intervened by tutoring this child after school to ensure he excelled in my exam class. But I didn't question the structures at play sufficiently.

By the time I was appointed as a senior leader, the school was in special measures. It was time for tough conversations. Challenging low expectations of teachers became a regular activity. I heard many narratives of White Privilege from teachers who had been using systems of narrow achievement over all else: 'I'm not here to teach literacy. Qualifications will get them a job and that's far more important.' After insisting on rigorous marking, I asked one White teacher why children were not offered their books to take home. The teacher responded, 'Letting them take their books home is like giving your baby to a crack addict.' This last comment was said in front of a Black teacher who had previously been a student at the school. He laughed nervously but later told me it was good to hear this apathy be challenged.

I was called in a few times by Black colleagues and it was in these discussions that I became more aware of my own White Privilege and how it was affecting my work. Sometimes I was not sensitive to the load this put on Black colleagues or the power dynamic of a colleague being the only Black person in the room when discussions were had. I would do things differently if I had my time again.

As a coach

I have coached a number of Black and Brown female leaders in education as they have found the language to talk about their lived experience following the murder of George Floyd and the increase in public discourse on anti-racism that followed. Having begun my own anti-racist work, I now try to hold the space cleanly. On one occasion, I felt excited that anti-racist work happening within the coaching space could effect structural change. This (again) was misplaced White saviourism. Structural change happens when we systematically challenge structures within and around us and do not put the responsibility for change on Black, Brown and racially minoritised people. Learning takes practice.

I believe that the magic of coaching can really help us all 'know our shit'. I work with a diverse range of leaders and feel strongly that collaboration with allies is essential to structural change. Having Black people in my social sphere who are willing to talk to me about race, as Professor Paul Miller once taught me in some leadership training, has helped me to keep listening and to speak up.

Many White people are terrified of getting it wrong; they dissolve in apathy, anger or overwhelm, or they use their privilege to avoid, take a break and get distracted by something else because they can (using sentences which gaslight and negate like those that start with 'Racism aside...'). White people have been winning unfairly for over four hundred years. It's not about getting it 'right'. It's about trying. Constantly. If we are to believe in positive change, we have to start with ourselves.

Change is a messy business – to believe in it starts with you. This is what it means to be an educator and a coach. Courage is not the absence of fear, but the willingness to act in the face of it (Kendi, 2019).

Good coaches and educators are usually fresh from ongoing personal change and learning through continuing professional development, which helps them to believe in what they do. Lasting positive sustainable change according to Chamine (2012) is 20 per cent insight and 80 per cent action. If reading this book and the literature referenced adds to your insight, what four actions can you take to ensure this insight becomes practice and change? Try writing these four steps down below.

1.

2.

3.

4.

Katie Friedman is the director of Gold Mind Neurodiversity Training Ltd, which provides neurodiversity training for leaders, educators and coaches. She is also a school leadership coach and a specialist trained ADHD coach.

Summary

Key learning points

- Listen to the experiences of pupils and staff in your school. What are their experiences of racism? Take prompt action to bring about change and ensure this is not only seen but also felt.
- Don't just focus on incidents of overt racism. Think about how you can challenge covert racism too: how does this manifest in your school and what needs to be done to change this?
- Work regarding anti-racist practice takes time and commitment. It is revealing, uncomfortable and confronting – but necessary.
- Black, Brown and racially minoritised folk have carried the burden for too long. True solidarity is needed for effective and long-lasting change.

Key question

Do you have an anti-racist policy in your school?

a) Yes

b) No

c) I'd better get on it!

Further self-reflection questions

1. How have you changed for the better within the last academic year?
2. How comfortable are you with failing and trying?
3. Do you believe other people can change?
4. What help do you need to be anti-racist?

Discussion points for staff meetings

- Do you think it is necessary to have an anti-racist policy in your school? Or is it enough that race is referenced as a protected characteristic in the Equality Act 2010?

11 Decolonisation of the curriculum

'A people without the knowledge of their past history, origin and culture is like a tree without its roots.'

Marcus Garvey

In June 2019, I attended an event at the University of Bristol which looked at the history of Bristol and its relationship with the slave trade. It was fascinating; I began to discover more truths about Bristol's history. We also had the honour of listening to Adrian Stone, Caribbean genealogist and founder of Own History, who talked about the importance of tracing your personal history and discovering who you are. Adrian talked about the disconnect that many Caribbean people face due to slavery and poor migration records.

Adapted from Barbados Slave Register 1834, Volume 11, pp. 54-59 [fo.28.30] ft. Nicholas Plantation 3rd March 1834.

One of the professors with whom I was grouped talked so proudly of his history. He could name generations and generations. He knew exactly who he was and what his family had contributed to the world. I looked at him in awe. That awe quickly turned to pain. I couldn't help but think: why does he get to know his history and I don't? The answer to that was simple. My history was stolen.

I had always questioned my history. I had always wondered who we were before we got to Jamaica. But all I've found is brick wall after brick wall. I spoke to my grandparents but their knowledge and history were limited and also very traumatic and triggering to discuss.

In a recent conversation with my grandmother, she talked about the beauty of Jamaica. Her face lit up, as she told tales of swimming in the river and picking fresh mangos from the tree. 'Aisha, you have never tasted anything like it.' She talked to the seasonal food that was on offer: guineps, pineapple, fresh coconut – the list was endless. I listened as her eyes glazed over, as it dawned on her that was home. A place she never wanted to leave. But she was sent for, as her parents were sold a dream, a Commonwealth paradise abroad, where they would be freezing cold and subject to endless racial abuse, and would never again return to the warmth they called home.

Yet I was hearing much of this for the first time. At the age of 36. Why did I not have this history before? Why didn't I learn more about my heritage and culture at school? Why was I subjected to a condensed and superficial view of my history, one which only extends to sporting heroes and civil activists? Where was the rest?

What do we mean by 'decolonising the curriculum'?

When we speak about the decolonisation of the curriculum, what do we really mean? The intention to 'decolonise the curriculum' has been discussed, debated and promised so often that perhaps it's lost its meaning and become another buzz phrase, an aspirational term that so many people wish to achieve. It is certainly an extremely academic term and is mostly referred to in the context of higher education. However, other phases of education are keen to get involved and ensure that they too have taken the opportunity to decolonise their curriculum. But what concerns me is that while many educators are using it as a term of educational progression, in reality, they have no idea what it means.

So, what does it mean?

First, we must look to the word 'decolonise'.

Decolonise: (of a state) withdraw from (a colony), leaving it independent. (Oxford Dictionaries)

When talking to schools, I challenge the educators I am working with to really think critically about the word 'decolonise' and to define what it means to them in the context of their curriculum. To decolonise the curriculum means to question the point of view that history is coming from. It is to review our colonial understanding and examine what it is we understand to be the truth. At its heart, it's about dissecting the narratives that we tell and the apparent baton of truth that we continue to pass down through the generations.

However, to truly decolonise, we are not just referring to the spaces and the curriculum that we teach. We are also referring to our minds. The coloniser and the colonised, the inferior and the superior, them and us. This reminds me of the famous line in the film version of *Matilda* when Matilda's dad tells her, 'I am smart, you are dumb. I am big, you are little. I am right, you are wrong, and there's nothing you can do about it.' But the time has now come for us to do something about it. It is time for us to challenge the narratives that we give to our children. It is time to recognise and realise that Black and Brown people are the majority on the planet. But the curriculum tells a different story. When we look at the curriculum that is being taught, you would think that Black and Brown people were almost non-existent. We are surrounded by our colonial past and it impacts on every aspect of our lives. It is only when we start to recognise this that we can begin to look at the school curriculum through a more critical lens.

Our current curriculum is arguably an act of omission. Black, Brown and racially minoritised people – People of Colour – are ignored and treated as if they've made no contribution to the world. Children can tell me who Thomas Edison is, yet they have no idea who Lewis Latimer is. Children can tell me what Robert Perry discovered, yet they have no idea who Matthew Henson is. In primary and secondary schools, we are of course working within a set National Curriculum and we can therefore only do limited service to decolonising the curriculum at the current time. True decolonisation will not take place until the government dismantles the entire curriculum and rebuilds it through a new lens. In the meantime, what we *can* achieve in our individual school curriculums is diversification and the addition of representation. What is the picture that we are trying to paint?

Activity: Quick audit

Think about the curriculum you teach and complete the table.

What is in your curriculum?	Who is in your curriculum?	Does it reflect the community you are serving?

What is happening in higher education?

Higher education is leading the way in efforts to decolonise the curriculum. There is still much work to be done, but without a centralised national curriculum, universities have the scope for more independence when it comes to bringing about curriculum change. In this first lived experience piece, we will find out more about what is happening in higher education. Think about what we could take away from this for schools.

Lived experience: Foluke Adebisi, Senior Lecturer, The Law School, University of Bristol

Can there be epistemic justice in the university's orchard?

The lack of representation of people racialised as non-White in UK higher education (UKHE) often makes headlines. These headlines are usually greeted with shock and surprise, especially when the data is disaggregated to highlight the sharp disparities experienced by members of UKHE racialised as Black. Yet not much changes. In 2021 – despite universities' vocal support for schemes including acknowledging how they have benefited from the trade in enslaved Africans, 'decolonising the curriculum', widening participation, supporting Black Lives Matter, and engagement in supposedly inclusive events like Black History Month – the data tells us that representation in UKHE is still elusive. Among other things, this sort of lack of representation results in and from 'epistemic injustice'. Epistemic injustice, in this sense, includes the silencing of a people's reality, their systemic exclusion from the mainstream, misrepresenting of who they are in truth, undervaluing their contributions to knowledge, life and society, as well as an ingrained distrust of them.

Universities' activities have not translated to a significant decrease in the awarding gap, a decrease in the ethnicity pay gap, a significant increase in the number of Black women in the professoriate, or an improvement in the funding pipeline. To unpick these issues further:

- In 2015–16, 78.4 per cent of White students were awarded a First or 2:1 degree, compared with only 66 per cent of Asian students and 53.1 per cent of Black students (Advance HE, 2017).
- In 2018, there were just 25 Black British female professors across all UK universities (Rollock, 2018).
- Funding problems meant that over a three-year period only 1.2 per cent of the nearly 20,000 studentships awarded by all UK Research and

Innovation research councils went to Black or Black Mixed students, and only 30 of those were from a Black Caribbean background (Advance HE, 2020a; Advance HE, 2020b; Leading Routes, 2019).

The lack of representation in the academic staff body of universities is also replicated in absences in university curricula. These absences have resulted in the proliferation of numerous student-led movements to diversify or decolonise syllabuses at universities in Oxford, Keele, London, Kent, Leicester, Bristol and other UK cities.

The university as the commons

The lack of representation in UKHE raises a recurring question about the role of universities in society. Furthermore, it is not just the low level of diversity that is concerning, rather who exactly is poorly represented at university. The lack of representation of people racialised as non-White and people from economically disadvantaged backgrounds (and the intersection of this with other axes of disadvantage) suggests that universities' curricula may be directed away from these absences. If the university is replicating advantage, can it really study the world around it? This situation has caused Morrow (2009) to describe universities as 'bastions of privilege… constitutionally unresponsive to some major social needs and mired in the complacency of the powerful'. However, universities still occupy a position of possibility, as can be evidenced by many areas of transformative activity. Universities still have the opportunity to curate knowledge for societal growth and change. The world is faced with problems such as racial injustice, severe inequality, extreme global poverty and environmental devastation, among others. For solutions, we look to policymakers… as well as academics who have studied these problems so that they can give informed advice to policymakers. However, the lack of representation in university spaces narrows down not just the faces that we see doing this work but more importantly the knowledge that is being deployed, developed and transmitted to each generation. The university as the commons has not always been welcoming to all forms of knowledge. The lack of representation suggests that the current welcome remains entangled in historical negation. The university is still not the commons it could be.

Towards epistemic justice

Many of those discarded forms of knowledge found themselves reduced to myth during periods of enslavement and colonisation – myths that were predicated on using epistemologies to racialise certain populations as inferior. Therefore, the movement toward 'epistemic justice' – turning away from the effects of hierarchical humanity and knowledge – has been called 'decolonisation'. Decolonisation, in that sense, has a particular register that extends beyond embodied representation. It requires universities to be intentional about engaging with Britain's history of very active participation in enslavement and colonisation, as well as the complicity of academics and universities in enabling, benefiting from and not properly acknowledging that history. Decolonisation is also about unveiling how and why diverse knowledge and epistemologies, ways of knowing and being known, are being kept out – as well as the effect this has had on actual people. Scholars who have written about epistemics – the superiorisation of one body of knowledge to eliminate others – have emphasised the need for us to confront this history and the complicity of universities in normalising and (still) reproducing this hierarchisation of knowledge (Grosfoguel, 2013).

It is suggested therefore that the desire within UKHE to acknowledge their entanglement, for example, with the trade in enslaved Africans instead only serves to centre universities in what should be a more horizontal conversation. While universities in the Global North should definitely be encouraged to assess what they *gain* and continue to gain from enslavement and the trade in kidnapped Africans, this process does nothing to assess what Africans and African-descended people have *lost* and continue to lose to enslavement, colonisation and the epistemologies that set these in motion and that were set in motion by them. Any research that focuses only on what a single university has gained (or gains) in purely financial terms completely looks away from the harm and reifies the Global North (and its universities) at the centre of the world. Such work essentialises 'bad people' and ignores the system, structure and epistemologies that enabled the harm that was and is racialisation and anti-Blackness. This sort of approach relies on the same epistemologies that hierarchised humanity to reverse the process. 'How long do we keep pointing out the bad apples, ignoring the fact that the orchard was planted on a mass grave? … and that we planted it there?' (Myhre, 2018)

Yet the university remains a place of possibility. There is still a lot that academics within UKHE can do to ensure representative bodies *and also* representative epistemologies. What if, over the next couple of years, universities built a body of scholarly work describing how colonial legacies and legacies of enslavement are reproduced in different areas within UKHE disciplines, within, for example, law, history, medicine, economics, literature, sociology, sports science, anthropology, artificial intelligence, environmental science, philosophy, international relations, politics, biology, and so on? What if academics put all this research into their curricula? What if they showed to students, in very concrete terms, exactly how the past bleeds into the present, how we walk side by side with history's ghosts, how we breathe coloniality every day, how our collective history is literally present in every single thing we do? What if UKHE becomes the commons it is truly meant to be? What if *all* the world's problems were the equal priority of UKHE? It may seem impossible. But, for now, the university remains a place of possibility.

Foluke Adebisi *is a university lecturer at the Law School, University of Bristol. She is also a writer, spoken word poet, and blogger. She blogs about her work on her website 'Foluke's African Skies'.*

Where do we begin with decolonising the curriculum in schools?

As educators, we need to acknowledge the position of power that we have. It is too easy to say that we can't work towards decolonising the curriculum because we have to teach based on exams or because we follow a particular curriculum. Whether we are the leader of our classroom or the leader of a multi-academy trust, we have the power to impact and influence the education and learning that will take place.

We have to first acknowledge our humanity. This is crucial to becoming anti-racist and ensuring we are delivering anti-discriminatory practices. This takes work. We must become aware of our own authority and appreciate the limitations that we place on ourselves and others. We must also accept that we do not know everything and that the process requires the unlearning and learning of new information together. In this way, we can learn together with the children we are educating. To do this we relinquish the power and remove the hierarchy that exists, and we remove ourselves from the place of domination. We can then become vulnerable and open ourselves to the possibility of a new truth.

What follows is an acceptance and knowledge that supports the ambition, which is of course self-actualisation: the ability to be seen for who we are through all of our wonderful lenses, whilst providing the same for the children we serve. When we have done this work within ourselves, we can begin to explore a concrete process to move towards a more representative curriculum, as described by Amy Saleh in her piece below.

The process of decolonising the curriculum

Over the years as an educator, I have experienced moments that triggered in me a sense of shame and humiliation, along with a growing realisation of the ironic miseducation of students by the education system. One moment that stands out in memory is during a lesson where I was teaching Beverley Naidoo's *The Other Side of Truth* and an eager student raised their hand to exclaim, 'Did you know that England is the most civilised country in the world?' I was caught off guard. After registering the comment and rapidly considering all my potential responses, I decided to pause the lesson and generate a discussion about the word 'civilised'.

Another moment was looking at an extract from Benjamin Zephaniah's *Refugee Boy* and realising that my students thought people in Africa didn't have televisions. When I projected images of vibrant African cities onto the whiteboard, they were stunned. However, impromptu educational moments like these are as useful as throwing tiny orbs of light into a gaping, shadowy chasm. It will take the concerted effort of all educators at all phases to confront rather than preserve harmful narratives about minoritised groups. We all need to respond to the calls to decolonise the curriculum.

So, what does this actually mean?

Essentially, it is a process that begins with an understanding of how Western concepts and ideas have shaped various observations and illustrations of the world. Removing this colonial lens requires intentional effort, which includes:

- being critical of information presented as factual
- being critical of prevailing, mainstreamed narratives
- ensuring history is told as accurately as possible, without omissions
- learning and self-reflection.

These suggestions are far from exhaustive but are essential elements of the process. I call it a process because, just as it takes time to build knowledge and construct mindsets, it will take continued unlearning and deconstructing, particularly of our own biases, to engage in decolonising work effectively.

Here are some ideas as to how schools might approach this work.

Representation Matters

Black History Month

Over time, the gradual inclusion of Black histories, narratives and contributions across the curriculum should mean there is no need for it to be pigeon-holed into one month, but for now it's worth thinking about how Black History Month might be approached. In 2014, an organisation called Word on the Curb released a short film called *What I Wasn't Taught in School*, featuring spoken-word poet Samuel King. It addressed the narrow approach to Black History Month, where the focus was typically slavery and the US Civil Rights movement. Though these are significant time periods and key figures such as Dr Martin Luther King Jr., Harriet Tubman and Rosa Parks played instrumental roles in the fight for freedom, Black history is far more expansive. Now there are countless resources online, ready and available for use in the classroom, whether it be directly from the Black History Month official websites or from other organisations like The Black Curriculum and BLAM (Black Learning Achievement and Mental Health).

The role of other curriculum subjects

Beyond PSHE (see Chapter 12), there are plenty of opportunities to get students thinking critically about the world around them.

In **English**, students could be led to consider the existence of the literary canon and to look more closely at whose voices are included and excluded. The English curriculum tends to feature writers who examine countries within the Global South from a Western perspective. Often these perpetuate mainstream narratives of people from the Global South as being uncivilised, unintelligent and poverty-stricken. Students need to be shown texts about the Global South written from the perspectives of the people who live there. When thinking about language, get students to scrutinise the notion of Standard English: how did it become standardised and by whom? What stigmas are attached to non-standard English speakers and why? What is a mother tongue, and why were colonial subjects forbidden from speaking theirs?

In **media studies**, why not have your students study the cultural relevance of the film *Black Panther* and how it defied mainstream representations of Africa? They could discuss the inclusivity – or exclusivity – of things like the Academy Awards.

In **creative arts**, students might learn about the appropriation and repatriation of historical artefacts, or discover the origins of rock and jazz music and how the economic proceeds of these art forms did not always benefit the communities from which they originated.

Science, technology, engineering and maths (STEM) offer the chance to contest racist ideas about intelligence and the impacts of the eugenics movement, while also looking at the numerous contributions from People of Colour which have led to ground-breaking discoveries, past and present.

In **humanities**, students can learn about the bountiful natural resources of the Global South and how different people lived before the colonial period. Disparities in wealth between the Global North and Global South can be inspected to challenge reductive dichotomies of 'rich' and 'poor' or 'developed' and 'developing' countries. This could lead into an investigation of the deceitful nature of international aid and the complicity of the Global North in the underdevelopment of the Global South.

There are many ways to decolonise the curriculum and these are just a few ideas. As educators of future generations, it is our moral and ethical responsibility to investigate the facts. Presently, we have novels and textbooks that have been written based on the biases and prejudices of society, not mere individuals. We have untruths, misrepresentations and suppressions of facts that have infiltrated a curriculum that has been in place for decades. In light of these 'revelations', we have no excuse to claim ignorance. Let's flip the script!

Amy Saleh is a GCSE English lecturer at an FE college. She has taught English for eight years and completed an MA in English Education in 2020. The focus of her thesis was anti-racism, anti-Blackness and the English curriculum.

Lived experience: Tracy O'Brien, head of history

I like to imagine how exciting it must have been. To have been around in the late nineteenth century when the Pan African movement began to grow in England. There was a growing belief that all people of the African diaspora had a shared past and possibilities for their shared future. It was the beginning of a movement seeking to promote unity and progress worldwide. Even before the Titanic had set sail or the Wright brothers had taken flight, intellectuals of African descent were publishing studies and news reports as well as challenging governments at home and abroad, sharing knowledge on how best to support building education and business. But this is looking through my rose-tinted glasses. How long had Henry Sylvester Williams, who set up the African Association in London in 1897, been struggling to progress this movement? What responses did he receive from his colleagues? How comfortable was it for him when he shared his views in his community? How far did he even share his thoughts? How did he find somewhere he belonged, somewhere he felt bold enough to take the steps in creating an ethos that later attracted Malcolm X, Kwame Nkrumah and Haile Selassie?

Meaningful curriculum change in my history classroom sometimes felt like starting a worldwide political movement. It can be challenging to know where to start and access the information you need, even though you know it is out there, somewhere.

The place I needed to look all along was outside the curriculum. My home city of Bristol was encouraging teachers and educators to work together to help make the curriculum more reflective of the city. I got involved with a media collective, CARGO, and I began to advise them on their educational materials. I was able to work with members of my community, who were ready to use their skill set to address the problems of a restrictive, narrow representation of British history. A history that ignored the contribution of those from the African diaspora. Together we committed to creating lesson materials through a project that brought together poetry, visual artistry, storytelling, history, education and business principles. Our conversations were challenging and wide-ranging, acknowledging where we had to be uncompromising and where we could seek to find common ground with a new generation of teachers who wanted to share a richer understanding of the past. The process was nothing short of liberating. I had found the kinship and collaboration that Pan-Africanism had been set up to inspire.

In this sense, I had been very fortunate. Not all educators have access to supportive organisations and networks that allow this level of collaboration. However, working as an educator does usually go hand in hand with an enthusiasm for learning. I began researching time periods and characters beyond the requirements of the traditional history curriculum. Some characters were familiar – Mary Seacole, Queen Nzinga – and some unfamiliar – Dutty Boukman, Sam Sharpe. I immersed myself in events, individuals and places that were fascinating; the world of Nanny of the Maroons, training for guerrilla warfare in the mountains of Jamaica, leading a resistance against the British for nearly half a century. Led by deacon Sam Sharpe, the peaceful protest for improved working conditions became a well-organised revolt by 500 men and women. Removing the constraint of improving my lessons helped me feel excited; I just wanted to know more. As I learned more, my perspective was changing irreversibly. The story of Empire cannot be explained without the story of Nanny's resistance; it leaves half the story untold. What other stories of resistance have I not been told? Telling the story of abolition, where the British saved the people of the colonies, has long been seen as too simplistic. The addition of Sam Sharpe's report gives an international dimension, explaining how the British government functioned across the globe and the increasing challenges it faced. I was reframing my ideas about how to better understand the past – not how to better represent the past to be more inclusive.

This broad reading had deepened my understanding of the complex trade structures, Empire and war, which make up such a huge part of Britain's past. Where connections between my characters and British history went quiet, I researched further. Use a search engine to look for facts about Rosalind Franklin or Boudica, and you will return page upon page of useful articles by reliable media and history outlets. Do the same for Queen Nzinga and you will run into some difficulty; your research base will be much more restricted. My reward for persevering was the discovery of female scholars from the Caribbean, books by historians of the African diaspora that were totally new to me, but were well known and studied. I unearthed papers and studies that shed new light on parts of the past previously hidden for me.

The London Manifesto of the Pan African Movement in 1921 called for the right to education in self-knowledge. The time I spent on my own right to education has not changed my views about the importance of children seeing themselves represented in the curriculum. It has, however, strengthened my understanding of why this change is good for all children, regardless of their background. It simply helps my subject make more sense. My research has helped craft high-quality lessons; these lessons have historical material from a range of viewpoints, historians, countries, journalists and museums that children have never interrogated before. Extracts from the Jamaican *Gleaner* sit alongside work by historians Verene Shepherd and CLR James. These advantages help future-proof the curriculum; why would anyone not want to teach these lessons when they bring so much? There is always more work to do, and I am always frustrated with the timescale. This method is slow, and its audience is somewhat restricted. However, the change does have long-lasting effects. I will not return to using restricted sources, and my students cannot unread or unsee the past as interpreted by members of the African diaspora.

Ultimately, we are all a product of the education we have experienced. The CARGO lessons I have helped create are beautiful: visually powerful, carefully constructed and laid out, and including poetry that enthrals students. They are all completely free to use and access. They have been created by a dedicated and hard-working team; by next year, everyone will be teaching these lessons at the secondary level.

Except that will not be the case, because as educators, we need to re-educate ourselves. If we are fortunate, we can do that with others who will help us move away from a Western view. If not, we can pursue this independently and share the process with our students. At the Pan African conferences, the delegates found that talk led to uncovering facts and purpose.

If you discuss the discoveries you make through your reading with your students, what do you think they would say? What if you just consistently talked about the silences you uncovered? What if you told them how it makes you feel as a teacher to educate them in your subject and feel like there is so much you haven't been taught?

We are at the start of meaningful curriculum change. It's an exciting place to be.

Tracy O'Brien is an educational consultant, secondary leader, writer and passionate historian. She is committed to revealing silences in our knowledge of the past and uncovering the stories that remain untold.

It's important to note that the British population is divided in their opinions about schools actively working towards anti-racist practice and diversifying the curriculum. Therefore, work of this nature doesn't come without risk to career, wellbeing and progression. There is the view that you are 'only doing this' because you are Black, Brown or racially minoritised yourself, or that 'you are woke' or 'this is political correctness'. The guidance from the government regarding 'political impartiality in schools' (Department for Education, 2022) has added fuel to these arguments. Therefore, it's essential to manage this work with care. My perspective is that I centre the work around safeguarding. No child should be unsafe in school because of the colour of their skin. Curriculum change works alongside pastoral support and diversifying the workforce to make the school environment safe for all students.

If we truly want to move forward with our curriculum, we need to think about the impact and the intention behind what we teach and how we teach. By doing this, we can move away from tokenistic moments such as Black History Month and instead create a curriculum so rich and diverse that Black, Brown and racially minoritised students will never again walk into a classroom, look at their skin and question: who am I? What have my people achieved? That is a classroom I would feel honoured to teach in.

Summary

Key learning points

When it comes to decolonising the curriculum, it is important to take a number of key steps:

- **Recognise your own advantage:** Having access to your personal history and stories may not be a privilege that your peers and many of your students have. Recognise the impact of this and the long-term implications for those who do not know their roots.
- **Understand where you are on your journey:** Are you adding representation and diversifying or are you decolonising and becoming racially literate?
- **Education:** Taking steps to educate yourself is crucial. There is a wealth of materials available for every learning style, from podcasts to books, from films to articles. It just takes an investment of time.
- **Check yourself:** Understanding your environment, bias, prejudice and privilege is extremely important. Knowing who you are will help you to do the work you need to do.
- **Reflection:** Time is needed for both you and your students to reflect on who you are. The more we do this work, the more we change and evolve. It is important to reflect on how far you have come and how much further you have to go. But the most important point to note is that the work will never be done.
- **Expand your sources beyond British, European and American scholars:** The works of these nations are more widely published and accessible, so it may be a quicker route. But what about the amazing sources of information from around the world that are being missed or overlooked?

Key question

When you were at school, how often did you see yourself reflected in your lessons?

a) In all my lessons
b) In most of my lessons
c) At certain times of the year
d) Never

What was the impact of this on your identity? If you were the teacher in these lessons now, what would you do differently?

Further self-reflection questions

1. Are you aware of what may be considered to be racist or racialising behaviour in a learning context? For example, are you cutting particular students off? Do you allow students to challenge your teaching and present their worldview? Do you speak over students or expect students to be a spokesperson for an entire group?
2. Does your curriculum content preserve or challenge prevailing narratives about minoritised groups?
3. Whose knowledge is centred within your curriculum?
4. Whose stories and contributions are featured within your curriculum?
5. How do you use language when talking about minoritised groups?
6. What learning and training do you need to undertake in order to consolidate your knowledge and understanding as an anti-racist educator?

Discussion points for staff meetings

- Consider this quote: 'Until the lions have their own historians, the history of the hunt will always glorify the hunter.' Chinua Achebe When we continue to tell history from one perspective, it is only one perspective that we will ever learn. What is the perspective of history that you were educated with? Is it still fit for purpose?

12 PSHE

'Everybody is a genius, but if you judge a fish by its ability to climb a tree, it will live its whole life believing it is stupid.'

Albert Einstein

Where does anti-racist practice belong? Is it an extra-curricular add-on? Or is PSHE the place?

PSHE stands for physical, social, health and economic education, as described by the PSHE Association. It is also defined as such in government documentation (see, for example, Department for Education, 2020c). PSHE is a subject about the whole child; it's about more than academic ability. Social, emotional and moral understanding are crucial fundamentals of PSHE. The knowledge that students gain should prepare them to be global citizens and help them to develop resilience, understanding, confidence and self-esteem – and it will ultimately affect their life chances. It is not extreme to say that in some cases it could be the difference between life and death.

There are several definitions of PSHE. Many of these refer to the outcomes of PSHE, rather than the process. They often begin with phrases such as:

PSHE should provide knowledge…

PSHE should provide understanding…

PSHE should lead to confident, responsive citizens...

However, a more helpful definition may be the one quoted in Her Majesty's Inspectorate 1989 'Curriculum Matters' document on 'Personal and social education':

'Personal and social education is concerned with qualities and attitudes, knowledge and understanding, and abilities and skills in relation to oneself and others, social responsibilities and morality.'

Take time to consider what PSHE means to you. If a student asked you to explain what it meant, how would you answer? How would you explain the types of themes or discussions that they may have in a PSHE lesson?

After reflecting on the question above, find or take a picture that expresses what PSHE means to you. Ask your colleagues to complete the task too.

Next, facilitate an opportunity where you can all share your photography and express what the subject of PSHE means.

This task will provide a baseline interpretation and understanding of what you and your staff understand PSHE to mean.

You could also ask colleagues to consider the subject of race and ask them to RAG (red, amber, green) rate their understanding of the topic as well as how they could incorporate it into their PSHE teaching.

PSHE and anti-racist practice

PSHE provides a check and a balance, one that allows us to look back, challenge and ask: has society changed? Has it moved on? As I've mentioned, 50 years ago, when my great-grandmother moved to the UK for a better life, to 'do her bit for Queen and country', she and my great-grandfather were met with 'No cats, no dogs, no Blacks and no Irish.' How do you think this would have been addressed in PSHE lessons had they existed then? But my bigger concern is: how far have we progressed from then? What would we say and do about this in PSHE lessons now?

The **personal** aspect of PSHE is concerned with the knowledge of oneself: the notions of empowerment, self-belief, acceptance and determination. **Social** education focuses on interpersonal skills, attitudes and the ability to deal and cope with a number of situations. PSHE **health** education aims to support young people to make informed choices about their mental and physical health. It should empower students to understand what is normal for them and, if issues have arisen, to seek appropriate support when needed. Topics range from diet and exercise to cyberbullying and internet safety. **Economic** education explores money's role in our day-to-day lives and how personal finances can be managed effectively. Students learn about debt, the positives and negatives, and understanding what it means to be an entrepreneur versus working as an employee. It also provides an opportunity for students to explore several career choices and consider what steps they may wish to take in the future.

When applying this to the context of anti-racist practice, I see the personal aspect as a moment of self-discovery. Connection to one's identity and culture. Knowledge of oneself and a willingness to acknowledge the identities, culture and heritage of others. The social aspect should allow for understanding, compromise, empathy, emotional understanding and racial literacy. It should also provide an opportunity to consider values and attitudes and demonstrate a true connection with difference, beyond the basic notion of tolerance.

Lived experience: Amy Saleh, GCSE English lecturer, FE college

It is crucial that students are given a space to explore and discuss issues of race and identity. In PSHE, they are encouraged to talk about relevant issues that affect their lives, so why not talk about race? Being a life skills-based subject, PSHE allows us as educators to address and bring down any barriers that prevent students from understanding or engaging with one another on the topic of racial identity. The ease with which they converse about race will vary across different contexts, but the important thing is to facilitate these conversations. You may want to design foundational lessons that prompt discussions about the following questions.

- What are race and ethnicity?
- What is racism? Where does it come from?
- What is the difference between bias, prejudice and discrimination?
- What is representation and why does it matter?
- What language should we use or avoid when talking about race – and why?

Amy Saleh is a GCSE English lecturer at an FE college. She has taught English for eight years and completed an MA in English Education in 2020. The focus of her thesis was anti-racism, anti-Blackness and the English curriculum.

PSHE as it is versus how it should be

PSHE has always been referred to as the subject that nobody wants to teach; a filler subject – one that is added onto timetables to fill a gap or used as a lesson to pass the time… a quasi-enrichment activity. It's often seen as a fluffy subject of no value. 'Miss, do we have to have PSHE lessons?' For years the subject has been approached and taught so poorly that it has developed a bad name. Yet we know the teachings of PSHE are deep rooted in real-life experiences. PSHE, when handled correctly, has the power to dive into our emotions and present us with opportunities to express our truths and desires.

To achieve this, you need a whole-school approach to PSHE. A culture of understanding and connection should be the golden thread throughout the curriculum. The latest Ofsted guidance talks to the intent of the curriculum. So, what is the intent of the PSHE curriculum that we are delivering?

PSHE should be taught as discrete lessons, with every child getting access to these lessons. However, lessons are often ad hoc or they take the form of assemblies, circle or tutor time. Sometimes they're simply tacked on to other curriculum subjects such as humanities or included in commemorative celebrations such as Black History Month or Anti-Bullying Week. This approach needs to change. For PSHE to make a difference, it requires consistent teaching, adequate, focused time and trained specialists. As it stands, it's underrated, ill thought out, and barely statutory. This is hard to stomach at times, especially when it is the only subject that I teach. I have such a passion for it, yet I would find myself arguing every year to ensure that it had its place on the timetable. Soon after I transitioned into education from my legal career, I decided that I wanted to qualify as a PSHE teacher. It was not enough just to teach it as an extra. I wanted to truly understand the foundation and fundamentals associated with the subject.

Lived experience: Ronnie Kisubi, geography teacher and head of diversity and inclusion

As an educator, there is often the expectation that we can teach anything, particularly when it comes to PSHE. The subject is broad and can range from finances to mental health, sex education to bullying, cultural holidays to politics around the world. The list is endless and teachers provide this learning experience day in and day out. But, when it comes to race, racial bullying or anti-racism, these learning experiences either don't exist within that school environment or many teachers shy away from the subject and feel unsure how to deliver lessons on these topics.

Instead of this being a reflection of the individual who is uncomfortable, this should highlight a broader need to boost the confidence of staff in delivering the content to ensure that they do it justice for the students. I have witnessed sessions where the teacher did not feel comfortable or confident with the content they had to deliver and this led to the students receiving a basic and stripped-back version of the content, with little discussion time for questions and not much of an opportunity to break down any barriers. This can create what could easily be interpreted by students as a box-ticking exercise and highlight the lack of care or passion for the topic at hand. This can be more detrimental than not delivering the content at all.

To facilitate the most productive PSHE environment, where staff feel confident delivering inclusive content and students feel empowered with opportunities to ask questions, a different approach is required. Resources must be broken down to staff with clear instructions and training with an open forum format should be provided, to allow everyone to ask questions and feel supported in doing so. This should result in each adult delivering the sessions in the most effective way – a way that promotes healthy discussion between the adult and students.

Ronnie Kisubi is a geography teacher and head of diversity and inclusion who is making a secondary school in South East England a more inclusive place through elevating the experiences of our Black students and students of colour, teacher training, and diversifying the curriculum.

This is a subject that has the potential to challenge minds and open doors. PSHE should provide a holistic approach to what would otherwise be a diet of purely academic education. It is a subject that (when taught correctly) supports childhood development and understanding and provides a great opportunity to talk about race and identity, whilst implementing anti-racist education and racial literacy.

I didn't know it at the time, but it soon became apparent that if I wanted to ensure students were racially literate and had a good understanding of anti-racist practice, PSHE was going to be the place where I could make it happen. The government often use this subject to implement teachings such as the Equality Act 2010, British values, and more specific subject areas such as female genital mutilation (FGM) and the Prevent Agenda. But what damage could this do if not taught properly? What stereotypes could it reinforce?

While teaching about these topics created fear in many educators due to the lack of training and support provided, I saw it as a golden opportunity to challenge the status quo and ensure that lessons regarding the understanding of FGM were handled with the most respect and understanding, whilst ensuring that children and their families were safeguarded during the process. Unlike the experience I had when I was at school. I always remember being taught about China. I must have been about ten or 11 at the time. We were shown a book with pictures of babies with bound feet and were told that their baby girls went in the bin. I look back now and I am horrified by the knowledge that was given to me and upset by the trauma that the one Chinese student in our class must have felt.

Without PSHE, where would children and young people truly gain the opportunity to explore who they are and what they believe?

Lived experience: Ruth Butler, deputy head, pastoral

I'll never forget the moment I realised that it quite literally doesn't matter what aspirational grades, predicted targets and performance-related assessments were constructed for the young people I stood across a room from each morning. It was like seeing the dust particles that only reveal themselves when the sun shines, and fruitlessly trying to brush them out of your vision.

Somehow education had fallen hard and fast into its own pitfalls of fixed mindsets and rigid expectations, of social norms – all in a time that was evolving at a breath-taking pace. I sat in a room surrounded by my peers, quite taken aback that the measure of our value, purpose and strength as the facilitators of young minds was 100 per cent validated by examined children meeting the algorithm-approved grades decided at the start of a school year.

Now this was a year where there were school pregnancies, children involved in sexual exploitation and children dancing around the edges of serious jail time. These children sat next to their peers, some of whom had walked to school for over an hour, dropping off each of their siblings along the way, and others who relied on school to wash their uniform and provide them with a hot meal.

Now don't get me wrong, at that age academic currency is golden. The exchange of knowledge and attainment really does open doors and life opportunities that can be transformative – there is no doubt about it. But somewhere in the back of my mind I remember being challenged about my fixed mindset on university courses. I had a teacher who reminded me that whilst getting good grades was nice, if a doctor was going to take care of you, they also needed to be friendly, empathetic and have some knowledge of real life outside of textbooks. And that's the reality. Knowledge might be power, and attainment might open doors, but it only does so much in the holistic growth of what life is really about – living.

Let me give you an example – I might not have enjoyed maths or been the strongest at it. In the couple of decades since achieving my all-important GCSE, I have used this qualification currency three times, and all for academic purposes. In real practical life, I have very little application for trigonometry or Pythagoras, and I don't have a clue where to start with my taxes. At 16 it was a key to a very specific door; I'm pushing 40 and technology has quite literally provided a very effective band-aid for my mathematical deficits in pretty much everything.

And there lies the rub: in the moment, as educators, we're preparing students for 'the world of work', for 'life beyond school' and to be 'employable characters'. The real question should be: are we preparing people? People who can grow, adapt and change? There is no denying that a global pandemic shifts a mindset with more precision and speed than most would predict or expect. If we truly think about the moments from which we evolve as people, they factor a few components: a demonstration of resilience, self-awareness and a degree of resourcefulness.

As educators we have to ask ourselves – what are we actually trying to achieve? Are we trying to share the content and knowledge of a book or syllabus, or are we fostering a love of learning and a thirst for the unknown? Never one to miss an opportunity for a good quote or platitude, I put to you that the real purpose of education is to teach someone to fish: that way, they have the tools, skill and knowledge to do it for themselves. What this really means is that education isn't about imparting what we know; it's about training and facilitating the real concepts of what it means to be collaborative, resourceful, adaptable and creative. These are traits that are transferable in the face of a diversifying global workforce.

'Education' used to be a place that guaranteed access to key social constructs. What 'education' has slowly begun to realise is that social constructs have evolved in the face of global crises and exponential self-awareness and growth in industries worldwide – something educators have known for a long time. 'Education' cannot adequately impart knowledge in preparation for the workplace because there are jobs that just don't exist yet. Historically, the foundations of education were to prepare for set industries, to work was once a 'career' or 'vocation', and now it is far more common to switch sectors three or four times before you're 30. If the pandemic hasn't shifted this into sharper focus, I don't know what will. We're watching offices, industries and entire sectors evolve or diminish as people are forced to isolate and withdraw to their homes for safety.

This takes us right back to the beginning. We have social constructs that require us as people to behave, act, follow or lead in specific ways. Community norms and social expectations require an acceptance and an ability to willingly engage in this construct. For too long, we've placed an emphasis on the currency of education, rather than a child's ability to access what's in front of them. By consistently asking young people to conform whilst they are developmentally vulnerable is risky… yes, it did us no harm… and yet, we're the very ones developing the technologies that are diminishing social interactions and encouraging social validation through screens. Einstein had it spot on about treating the monkey, fish and elephant the same when it comes to their ability to climb a tree. If we expect our algorithms and academic expectations to be the only things working for young people, our success rate is going to be significantly lower than we want it to be. Good luck in your professional aspirations for validation.

Work through this with me…

There's a child whose morning started at 5am with their youngest sibling because their mother is at work. They live a five-minute bus journey away from school but because mum's not home yet they've got to wait, and then they have to take their two younger siblings to school before they reach your door… so the real question is: are you going to challenge them for forgetting their equipment – it's policy; it's how we raise standards – and when they can't stay late for the extra sessions to move their borderline grades because they're back on the school run, how do you explain yourself to the head?

We provide a service to meet the needs of young people, without actually considering the context of what that really means for them, and there is a basic assumption that parents will fill the gaps, without considering their individual learning, economic or social profiles. The expectation that parents fill the void between the classroom and life outside the school gates is dangerous for our young people in that our community expectations have shifted along with our priorities about what is important.

So how does context bring our real intentions and expectations into sharp relief when we're really at the chalk face with our young people? The duality of imparting knowledge alongside preparation for life is complicated. We know that academic currency opens doors, but we also know that walking through the doors and embracing what's on the other side (once you've chosen the right door, that is) is far more complex, especially when you're a child.

PSHE has long been a band-aid to 'cover the gap'. It's the first place people look to when children have acted poorly…

- Did they get taught about the behavioural expectations before you told them off?
- How do you know they understood that mistreating people who are different to them is actually an act of discrimination if it comes from a place of prejudice?

It's also the place that we look to when it goes horribly wrong and our safeguards fail…

- Do they know what abuse of trust is?
- Are you sure they understand how to seek active consent in their relationships?

In England it is a legal responsibility for all staff to have read and understood 'Keeping children safe in education' (Department for Education, 2021c), which outlines all the contextual safeguarding areas where children could be exposed to harmful, risk-taking or abusive behaviours. The introduction of 'peer-on-peer' abuse is a direct result of children mistreating other children. The fight in the playground is no longer just that. Our social and societal values, and that preparation for living, are beyond preparation for work. There has been so much educational focus on the 'working' part of growing up and knowing how to do a job that we've forgotten that life is living. That means understanding how to thrive rather than survive, knowing how to adapt and transform through seasons of life, and finding healthy methods and strategies to cope.

How do we deliver in our legal safeguarding responsibilities without PSHE? How do you take a group of young people and lift the veil on the complexities of living? How do you put a group of young minds in a room and really unpick subject, opinion, values and fact, when their contextual mindset exists through a filter of their experience and nurture? How do you break through long-established views around gender, sexuality and intimacy to enable children to develop positive, socially adaptable mindsets when faced with their first relationship, their first moment of intimacy, their first foray into debt, their first moment of discrimination, their first moment of self-doubt, the first time they realise they can't get out of bed…

PSHE is a space where your environment matters. The values of the place you're in matter before you walk through that door. We're asking young people to think about a world they haven't yet stepped into or make decisions that aren't needed in the immediacy. You're also asking young people to care about their world and values within the context of their broader communities. We ask ourselves why people 'troll' each other online, why people hide behind extremist views, why people struggle to feel good enough in themselves. So, in the world of PSHE, we create a space to explore, examine, analyse and reflect without fear of shame or judgement. The child who learns they don't have to rush into sexual intimacy on a first date might take their time to get to know someone before they allow themselves to be physically vulnerable. The child who learns to assess their baseless opinions of others before sharing them may not be faced with challenges of discrimination around sex, gender or race. The child who learns to consider all their options before acting may be less risk-prone when it comes to substance use and misuse. And that child – who isn't heartbroken, or carrying an STI, or being sanctioned for discrimination or taking drugs – might just be the one who turns up and tells you they're having a bad day and that they don't know how to cope. How do you prioritise an A grade over a mental health crisis? You wouldn't and you couldn't. The lack of statutory PSHE for so many years has left schools having to prioritise league tables instead of the whole pupil, what their needs are before they turn up to the classroom, and their individual, contextual challenges – and this is true for children in all walks of life.

Without PSHE a child is rarely placed in a safe environment with the time, space and expertise to really challenge their perceptions of themselves and others. Thinking beyond their own borders and what it means to be a 'citizen' globally, nationally or locally, how does a child know they feel seen – be that physically, emotionally, culturally or socially? If we're looking to address the challenges of identity within a community and cultural norms between groups, where better to put it than in a PSHE lesson? Quality PSHE means addressing the sensitive nuances required to be open and vulnerable about 'trigger' topics such as race, gender and sexuality. In fact, the entirety of the Equality Act 2010 can be discussed, unpicked and understood. Everyone has an opinion – not everyone has the capacity or language to know how to share it. This is how children get lost in extreme and polarised viewpoints in a world flooded with misinformation and oversaturated with positions.

Quite frankly, it doesn't matter what academic currency you hold if you don't know what to do with it. It's like winning the lottery and then spending decades unsure what to spend your first penny on. PSHE is broad, all-encompassing and covers a multitude of academic sins. It's been weakened and disempowered because of bias and prejudice – it's seen as a soft subject that 'you don't do exams in anyway'. But if you have a real grasp of PSHE, you understand that it's the pin code to the ATM where all your money is stored – and you'll know exactly where to make your first 'purchase' when the time is right.

Ruth Butler is deputy head, pastoral, designated safeguarding lead and head of PSHE. Across all her roles, she explores pupil wellbeing as the source that enables pupils to lead fulfilling lives.

PSHE and the hidden curriculum

PSHE teaching is not simply what happens in the classroom. It should include what is known as the 'hidden curriculum'. This is the curriculum that is modelled by everyday interactions between students, the way in which teachers handle incidents, the way in which students are spoken about and the support that is provided to those who need it most. For example, a student is called the N-word in class. How does the teacher decide to deal with it?

- Park it.

- Address it there and then.

- Ask the student who said it to step outside.

- Focus on the victim and ensure they are OK.

- Convince the victim that the person didn't mean any harm (gaslighting).

What impact would witnessing the above have on a student? If they see the teacher address it, what does that model do for students? If the teacher does not address it or says that the person didn't mean it, what message does it send?

Anti-racism education must be woven into the journey of a young person's educational experience.

In the United Nations Convention on the Rights of the Child (1989), articles 28 to 30 talk explicitly about the right to an education, that every child should reach their full potential and every child should have access to teachings related to their culture. Here is what these articles say in more detail:

Article 28 (right to education): Every child has the right to an education. Primary education must be free and different forms of secondary education must be available to every child. Discipline in schools must respect children's dignity and their rights. Richer countries must help poorer countries achieve this.

Article 29 (goals of education): Education must develop every child's personality, talents and abilities to the full. It must encourage the child's respect for human rights, as well as respect for their parents, their own and other cultures, and the environment.

Article 30 (children from minority or indigenous groups): Every child has the right to learn and use the language, customs and religion of their family, whether or not these are shared by the majority of the people in the country where they live.

These themes should be discussed at various phases of a child's education and should be in place to explore ideas and understanding. This should not be an optional choice, an educational add-on or an impromptu lesson to fill some time. Instead, it should be used to celebrate an array of beautiful cultures, to challenge discrimination and bias, and to understand connection and identity.

As educators we have a privilege and responsibility to ensure that we prepare students to become global citizens. However, this is not a 'nice to have'. Children have a right to this under the UN Convention. The hidden curriculum, PSHE and citizenship are vital components in ensuring that children and young people have all they need to be equipped. However, this will not happen just in the classroom. It will take place in tutor time, in the corridors, on impact days, through resources, through everyday interactions and through the collective culture and shared understanding that have been built in the school.

PSHE: reactive, proactive or both?

PSHE also plays a key part in the culture of safeguarding and is often used as a space to respond to current affairs or to trends picked up following safeguarding referrals. When considering racism and racist incidents, I believe they should be firmly positioned as an area of safeguarding that is monitored and data should be shared with staff and students.

Safeguarding is everybody's business and racism is something our children should be safeguarded against. Whilst PSHE should be a subject that supports proactive and preventative teachings and should help to reduce the exposure of harm that students are subjected to, PSHE can also be a place where reactive conversation can take place. When discussing racial incidents and victims of racist incidents, particular attention should be paid to Black, Brown and racially minoritised students, and adequate counselling support services should be available for students to access. The process can be triggering and traumatic; therefore it is important that signposting to external agencies is available for caregivers.

In the summer of 2020, following the Black Lives Matter marches and the taking down of the Colston statue in Bristol, I wrote an open letter to my colleagues. In it, I explained what it was like to be a Black person at that time. I expressed to them the racial trauma I was going through and triggering media I was exposed to on a daily basis. It was like picking a scab, again and again. And all I wanted to do was begin to heal.

This prompted me to generate a series of lessons: 'What is in race?', 'What is in activism?' and 'What is in allyship?' It was important for students to have the opportunity to discuss what these meant, whilst also providing the opportunity to understand historical contexts and present-day understanding. Students needed the opportunity to make sense of the world and process their thoughts and understanding.

It was surprising to hear from several children that they didn't know what race and racism meant. It was a surprise because the students were attending a school that had a predominantly Black and Brown population as well as very limited access beyond their local area, one which was also a community of Black and Brown people. Many of the Black students talked about race from an arm's length perspective – although they were Black and Brown, it wasn't their story. I questioned this; I wanted to understand more. Students spoke of slavery being their only connection to race and racism (understandable given the limited experiences of Black history in their curriculum). This left some children believing, thinking and feeling that it was not a story for them as students of African, Asian and White minority descent, rather a story about their Caribbean peers.

After hearing their view, I could understand why perhaps their understanding and experience of race and racism were different to mine.

I then spoke to a colleague from Ghana about this and he too expressed that race was not a concept he grappled with in Ghana. In fact, he grew up with an understanding of who he was. He knew his name, his lineage. He was a king and empowered and proud of his skin and heritage. Yet when he arrived in the UK, it didn't matter. He was Black. But this concept of Black was a new thing to him. He was always African; he was Ghanaian. But here, his identity was lost. He was now part of a homogenous group, and all Blacks were the same.

PSHE units on identity and culture

PSHE units on identity and culture provide the chance to create connection and understanding. Students can start from a place of confidence and pride rather than deficit. PSHE can be the perfect place to discuss racism and discrimination, and it can be used as a tool to combat and challenge racial incidents and create student solidarity. However, it can also be a place for the richness and culture of all students to be celebrated – after all that is the world that we want. Isn't it?

To achieve this, alongside reacting to incidents that occur either in school or in the news, PSHE lessons must be proactive in teaching about identity, culture and race. Units on these topics should be taught in every key stage to promote a sense of connection, understanding and belonging. This is a positive step you can take to embed inclusion in your school. Below are some suggestions for where conversations of race can be mapped to the PSHE curriculum, based on guidelines from the PSHE Association (2020).

KS1	Pupils…
	• begin to develop an understanding of what makes them special
	• explore the ways in which every person is unique
	• recognise their similarities and differences to others
	• think about the different groups they are a part of
	• learn about bullying:
	  • how people might feel if they experience hurtful behaviour
	  • reporting bullying and telling a trusted adult
	  • that offline and online bullying, teasing and name-calling are unacceptable.

KS2	Pupils…
	• explore their identity, individuality and personal qualities, through their ethnicity, family, gender, faith, culture, hobbies, likes and dislikes
	• recognise the importance of self-respect:
	  ◦ how this might affect their thoughts and feelings about themselves
	  ◦ treating others politely and with respect, both offline and online
	  ◦ building courteous and respectful relationships
	• develop their understanding of diversity and the benefits of living in a diverse community
	• identify the different groups that make up their local community and what 'community' means
	• examine stereotypes, the impact they can have on behaviours and attitudes towards others and what can be done to challenge them
	• consider the meaning of discrimination and how they can challenge it
	• learn to define prejudice, how to recognise discriminatory behaviours and actions, and how to respond to these if witnessed or experienced
	• learn more about bullying:
	  ◦ how to respond when they witness or experience hurtful behaviour offline and online
	  ◦ reporting concerns and seeking support
	  ◦ trolling and harassment.

KS3	Pupils… • develop their ability to promote inclusion and challenge discrimination in a safe way both offline and online • examine how peers can support each other to resist pressure and influence, challenge harmful social norms and access appropriate support • learn about the impact of stereotyping, prejudice, prejudice-based language and discrimination, including racism, faith-based prejudice, sexism, homophobia, biphobia, transphobia and ableism • learn to recognise and challenge family or cultural expectations that have the potential to limit aspirations • appreciate how all issues can be considered from a wide range of different viewpoints • develop their understanding of how extreme views can affect people's attitudes and beliefs • explore the impact of bullying in all its forms and develop skills and strategies to respond to bullying if witnessed or experienced.

KS4	Pupils: • explore strategies to challenge prejudice and discrimination in all their forms • develop the skills they need to provide support to younger peers over whom they may have influence • understand the importance of challenging stereotypes about career options, having high aspirations and seeking new opportunities • examine the way in which social media exaggerates and distorts information about situations or viewpoints and how this can influence perceptions of people and events • appreciate our shared responsibility around challenging extreme viewpoints that incite violence or hate.

PSHE lesson series: What is in a name?

In 2018–19, I developed and delivered a series of Key Stage 3 lessons for One Bristol Curriculum (www.onebristolcurriculum.org.uk) on identity and culture. These were called 'What is in a name?'. The lesson plan was born out of a conversation with my neighbour, Whisper. We had lived opposite each other for years and I believed Whisper was a nickname. Then one sunny afternoon as we were chatting, he explained that Whisper was his birth name. He told me that in Zimbabwe children were named after what their parents wanted them to become, and his grandfather wanted a quiet child. He went on to tell me that children would often be called things like 'Millionaire' and 'Precious'.

This got me thinking: what is in a name? How important is it to our identity? What about when teachers pronounce students' names incorrectly or refuse to pronounce them at all? I had an experience of this when a teacher asked if she could shorten my son's name from Tacari to Tac. I swiftly responded with a 'no' and stated that it was three simple syllables: Ta-car-e.

During the delivery of this project, students came forward and expressed to teachers that their names had been pronounced incorrectly for years. Some students expressed that the names we knew them by in school were abbreviated or whitewashed for the benefit of their teachers as it would be easier for them. What is the excuse for this? If we can teach children the periodic table, if we can learn about composers with names like Tchaikovsky, can we not take a moment to learn the names of our students?

Figure 12.1 *What is in a photograph?*

Figure 12.2 *What is in our dress?*

Figure 12.3 *What is in a song?*

This one lesson then led to a number of lessons exploring different identities and cultures. The three lessons were:

- **What is in a photograph?**

This lesson explored the importance of representation in the art industry by looking at the Seven Saints of St Paul's in Bristol: a series of painted murals by Michele Curtis depicting seven Black Bristolians. These Seven Saints were local heroes, known for their activism and for serving their communities through social work, nursing and healthcare. Each student researched the achievements of one of the saints, designed their own mural for the saint and then presented this to the rest of the class.

- **What is in our dress?**

This lesson explored the influence of African and Asian dress on fashion and the wider world. The students learn about the saree, the five Ks of Sikhism (the Kachera, Kesh, Kanga, Kirpan and Kara), Caribbean dress, Black Panther-inspired African fashion and West African dress. Each student was asked to bring in an item of clothing that represents them and talk about what it means to them and their culture.

- **What is in a song?**

This lesson explored the influence of music, the stories told and the emotions felt. Students learned about the influence of African and Caribbean music in current popular music, covering Reggae, Afrobeats and Blues. They listened to three songs with a connection to the African diaspora and identified the genre of music, the emotions of the song and its key message.

These lesson ideas should be adapted according to age group and context, but they centre around allowing students to celebrate themselves. When I delivered these lessons in two primary schools, I took some photos of the children's work and I have included a selection on pages 188 and 189 so you can see some possible outcomes.

Facilitating lessons about racism, race, culture and identity: some tips

- **Objective**: As you would in other subjects, set an objective for your lesson. Lesson objectives could include:
  - ○ What is prejudice, bias and discrimination?
  - ○ What is race?
  - ○ What is racism?
  - ○ What is meant by stereotyping?
  - ○ What is activism?
  - ○ What does it mean to be a bystander?
  - ○ What do we mean by culture?
  - ○ What do we mean by nationality?
  - ○ What do we mean by identity?
- **Define key words**: Provide a glossary for students to access, then provide them with an opportunity to write in their own words what the terms mean to them.
- **Timing**: Do not rush the lesson. Provide time for discussion and ask students to think about what they have witnessed or experienced.

- **Intent**: Be clear with the intent of your lessons. What do you want the students to know when you have finished the lesson?

- **Context**: Ensure that children and young people, particularly younger children, have a sense of the timeline. Do they understand the difference between the historical context and the present day?

- **Lived experience**: This is vital to the learning for all children and young people. Question their experiences and what they have witnessed.

- **Questioning**: Critical questions are key to test knowledge and understanding but also to test the temperature of the room.

- **Close the loop**: Go back to the beginning and test how far they have come with their understanding.

- **Nuance**: Explain that racism is not just overt and only by 'bad people'. It has become the acceptable norm in society. This is often expressed as soft, casual racism, which can manifest as microaggressions. It is also important to understand the impact of unintended harm: the fact something was unintended doesn't always lessen its impact. A great example of this is, if you accidentally pour hot coffee on someone, the natural response is not to say, 'Why are you upset when it wasn't my intention to pour a hot drink on you?' The more appropriate response is to acknowledge your mistake, apologise to the other person and move more carefully in future (Anderson et al., 2020).

- **Racial trauma**: Be aware that it may exist in your classroom. Talk to parents, carers and students who may have lived experience and may find the lesson triggering.

- **Cross-pollination**: Consider where conversations can take place across a number of curriculum areas concurrently, to provide context, different perspectives and a deepening of understanding.

- **Accurate history**: Make sure any history you are teaching is accurate and taught through different lenses. Take, for example, enslavement. Ensure it is not just told from the perspective of Black and Brown people's experiences. What role did White people play? It is uncomfortable to admit, but it provides an accurate depiction. Equally, when talking about the abolition of slavery, don't forget the Black revolutions. Black and Brown folk didn't just sit there waiting with open arms. They fought for their freedom.

Throughout all of this, it is crucial to remain aware and sensitive to those for whom this is not just a lesson, but a lived experience. It is important to be calm and reflective and allow challenges to take place. You need to then secure the students with a clear understanding of discrimination and racism and the settings' policy, practice and responses to these types of incidents. Depending on where you are in your journey, I always think it is a good idea to begin this process by ensuring children and young people have an understanding of their own identity and culture. Developing some 'What is in…' lessons relevant to your own cohort and local community would be a very useful place to start this work.

What if parents want to withdraw their children from PSHE?

During my time as an assistant principal, there were occasions when I had to talk to parents who wanted to withdraw their children from core elements of their education. In my experience, it occurred when parents wanted to withdraw their children from:

- relationships and sex education
- sessions regarding racism, Black Lives Matter and anti-racist practice
- sessions on the Prevent Agenda
- sessions on female genital mutilation (FGM)
- Christian celebrations when another religion was observed.

Often the fear was about converting: that the school would be a key instrument influencing their child's mind.

In most of these cases, my fellow educators were unsure about what they could do and would shy away and put the child in the library or another room. My approach, in the first instance, was to talk to the parent or carer. My first question would be: 'Can you please help me to understand what your worry is?' The answer was often: 'I do not want you to fill my child's head with ideas that are not in agreement with our values.'

A parent and carer will always have the final say in regard to PSHE-type lessons. However, in my experience, if parents can be shown materials, if they can understand the school's rationale, and if they are reminded of the school's values and principles, this can go a long way to breaking down barriers and encouraging the participation of their child in the learning. I often ran sessions where I would teach the lesson I was due to deliver to the parents and carers who had concerns. I only ever had one parent walk out of my lesson!

Summary

Key learning points

- It is vital that we appreciate the importance of PSHE and the role it plays in education. Students are much more aware of politics these days. Many of them have views and are not afraid to share them and act on how they feel. It is important that these conversations are addressed and that students feel that they are being acknowledged, listened to, consulted – and that feedback is acted upon.
- PSHE should be taught as discrete lessons, rather than taking the form of assemblies, circle time or an add-on in other subjects. Staff must be fully trained so they feel confident to deliver high-quality, inclusive content and promote healthy classroom discussion.
- Use PSHE as a space to react to current affairs and incidents that occur in school to support safeguarding, but don't forget that PSHE must also be proactive. In every key stage, units should cover identity, culture and race to promote a sense of connection, understanding and belonging.

Key question

Do you feel anti-racist practice has a place in PSHE?

a) Yes
b) No
c) Maybe

If yes, where would you place anti-racist practice within PSHE?

a) Personal
b) Social
c) Health
d) Economic
e) All the above

Further self-reflection questions

1. What is your childhood memory of PSHE?
2. What aspect of PSHE had the most impact for you?
3. When incidents of racism happen in the wider world, how do you discuss them with your students?
4. How do you prepare for the conversations?
5. What support do you have in place?
6. How do you address caregivers who wish to withdraw their students from PSHE?

Discussion points for staff meetings

- Several incidents have affected the world in the last 20 years. How did you address these incidents in your settings?

  a) 9/11 (11 September 2001)
  b) The Manchester Arena bombing (22 May 2017)
  c) The murder of George Floyd (25 May 2020)
  d) The Palestine–Israel crisis (2021)
  e) The murders of Sarah Everard and Sabina Nessa (2021)

- How were culture and race discussed in the context of the above events?
- How were students supported?
- What did you learn from the steps you took?
- If you were to address those incidents now, how would you handle them differently?

13 Parents and caregivers

'Fear-based parenting is the surest way to create intimidated children.'

Tim Kimmel (2005)

What is the role of the parent or caregiver? Should the school set the moral compass or does it start at home? It's an interesting question to consider. And what happens when a school's values and morals don't align with what a child is being taught at home?

During my interview to become an assistant principal, one of the questions posed to me was: 'What is it that parents and carers want from a school?' The simplest answer would be: a good education; the opportunity for their child to become the person they wish to be in the future; and all the career opportunities that the world can provide.

My answer was: safety.

As a parent of a Black child, my decision about which school to send my son to was based on whether he would be physically, emotionally and psychologically safe. When I started applying for secondary schools for my son, I had a set of key questions:

- What is the diversity of the leadership team?
- What is the diversity of the staff body?
- What mental health and wellbeing support do you provide?
- Can I see your equality, diversity and inclusion policy?
- Can I see your behaviour policy?
- What is attainment like amongst different ethnic groups?
- What is the ethnic make-up of the school?
- Can I talk to any students to hear about their experience?
- What Black history is taught? How is it taught? When is it taught?
- How do you handle racist incidents?
- What food do you serve?

My son hated this part, as I would get out my notepad and start writing down the answers. In most cases, I would be directed to go and read the website. A few would show me work in the students' books. But one school stood out to me – they turned the questions back on me and asked why I wanted to know all these things.

I expressed that it was simple. As a parent of a Black child of Caribbean heritage, I am aware that he is more likely to be policed in school, three times more likely to be excluded than his White peers (Department for Education, 2020a), less likely to be listened to, and more likely to be gaslit if he raises concerns. I continued, he is unlikely to be taught anything about Black history – other than slavery and perhaps some information on civil rights. That's why I needed to know how much additional work I'd need to do at home to ensure his safety.

The teacher was stunned at my response. But then they wanted to know more. What more could they do as a school to ensure that all children felt a sense of belonging? My answer, again, was simple: start with you.

Considering the needs of *all* parents

I recently came across a quote: 'Every home is a university and the parents are the teachers' (Mahatma Gandhi). As a parent or caregiver, you want to make the right choices for your children. You want to ensure that you impart knowledge that will prepare them for life. But what if your values and beliefs are not aligned with your child's school or perhaps with wider society?

My first experience of this as assistant principal was the work around Prevent. I became a Prevent trainer. I attended Scotland Yard and debated its purpose. I spoke with community groups. But what became apparent was that there was a singular government view about what should be taught. However, the reactions and experiences of our parents and caregivers would all be different because of what they had experienced – and primarily because of who they are.

Our White British parents saw no harm in Prevent. In fact for many, it was great; it would safeguard their children. But for my Black and Brown parents and particularly for parents who were of Islamic faith, it was a different story; they knew they would be targeted. No longer could they carry a bag on a bus or say the word 'bomb' or 'explosive' without someone second-guessing their motives. Every summer, a flurry of concern would be raised because some of these students would be travelling abroad and there would be a worry for their safety. But what about the other children? Would we be as worried if they were going on holiday? Would we be taking an interest in their faith or belief? It is clear that the White gaze determines who and what is a threat, and the way in which the Prevent Agenda surveillances and dehumanises Black and Brown people and those from Islamic communities is an example of this. As things currently stand, Prevent is a legal obligation in schools, but think carefully about how you are implementing it. Who benefits and who suffers as a result? Consult with parents from Black, Brown and Islamic communities and consider the impact on their children and their families.

Educating and informing parents to support anti-racist practices at home

Particularly in the Early Years and in primary education, parents should be encouraged to talk to children about their race, identity and culture and how to celebrate those around them. Often these topics are treated as a taboo. They are feared – as if talking about them at a young age will lead to division. It is the opposite. We see colour; we see and experience cultural difference. Addressing this from an early age means children will appreciate difference and consider this an abundance, rather than look at it from a deficit position of negativity. The book *My Skin, Your Skin* (Henry-Allain, 2021) is a helpful resource to suggest to parents to get them started.

In the following lived experience piece, Lucy Dixon will talk more about how parents can support anti-racist practices at home. Think about how you might support the parents of children in your class or school to implement some of the practical advice Lucy shares.

Lived experience: Lucy Dixon, parent specialist

When I was ten, I moved with my family from London to Yorkshire. I went from a large, culturally and racially diverse inner-city school to a tiny all-White village primary. I noticed the differences. I didn't say anything.

Within a year I started secondary school. My local comprehensive was a 50/50 mix of White and Asian kids. I experienced racism for the first time. I watched and listened as the White kids I'd just spent Year 6 with made racist remarks. I remember the shock and feeling sick. I didn't do anything.

When I look back on this time now, I can see that I didn't know what to do. I didn't understand White Privilege or the responsibility that comes with it. I, perhaps, did not believe that racism was real.

I was raised by parents who believed in equality, who celebrated different races and cultures in our home through music, art, food and books. But they didn't tell me that racism was real. They didn't teach me how to act when I saw it. And they didn't teach me (because I don't think they knew) that my Whiteness was a privilege that should be used to make change.

It is not enough to be anti-racist. To feel bad, but to actively do nothing, is to say that racism is OK. As a White person, my concern at saying something in the right way, so as not to offend, is pure privilege and is nothing compared to the fear and anger Black people experience every day.

And now I am a parent. I know how racist our world is, and I know how much I benefit from the system because of the colour of my skin. I see that it is my responsibility to pass this on to my children. I want them to understand their privilege, to feel confident to actively use it for good and to always be questioning the White rhetoric around them.

A large part of this is passed on by teaching that representation matters. I want my children to grow up seeing all kinds of people so that the differences are familiar and so they experience the facts and the beauties of other people's worlds. Having books and art and food around the home that includes different races and cultures brings conversation and challenge and lessons. It also means I can point out when it's not there. And we can consider the why, and what the impact is, and how it feels to never see yourself represented. And then they will spot it and I will encourage their observation and we will consider what could be done. And then, as young people and adults, it will be second nature to question racism and voice it. They will see it, like I did, and they will know what to do.

And whilst I know it is not enough to say, 'My child will never say anything racist', I also know now this statement isn't true. The very act of learning is to sometimes get it wrong. If my children are to explore race so that they understand, then they must be able to ask questions, to discuss and to make mistakes. Because calling out racism is hard. It is nowhere near as tough for me, as a White person. But to stand against systems or peers or family and say, 'That's not acceptable', and to take it further by explaining and modelling what is right? That takes more than simply knowing. As parents, alongside providing representation, we must give our children confidence in their voice, strength in discussion and a skin that deflects the words of people who are angry and fearful.

There are many everyday things we can do as parents to combat racism:

- Always challenge racist views out loud, whether from the media, family and friends or the system. Model to your children that you do not stand for it.
- The characters in your children's books and toys should represent different races, cultures and religions. The books your child reads

should be diverse in all these areas to normalise our differences and similarities.

- When colouring and drawing with your child, use different skin colours and tones, consider different hair types and explore different cultural dress.
- When you are consuming media where race isn't apparent, shine a light on it. Wonder aloud and discuss what this means.
- Celebrate discussion – make space for it in your home and offer your children praise for using their voice.
- Discuss different religious and cultural dates in your home. Find out what your children already know; if it's more than you, let them teach you.
- Bring a range of foods into your home. Try new things and wonder together about where foods come from, what this country has taken for its own and how essential food traditions are.
- Encourage and welcome your children's friends of all races. If you encounter some resistance, try harder. Other families may have had negative experiences before or may hold cultural beliefs that mean playdates need to happen differently.
- Sit with your older children and watch TV and documentaries that cover race. Discuss.
- Model respectful challenging: get your children used to not always being right, to encountering different opinions and to how to get their point across.
- Find out what your children's school is teaching in the syllabus. If it's not enough or only during specifically allocated time periods, such as in October for Black History Month, challenge this. Use your privilege to say you expect representation in what children are taught.
- If race hits the news, do not hide it. Be open and ensure your children understand it and will not gain further falsehood or White rhetoric.
- Connect action with thought and feeling. Talk through what someone must be thinking when they are racist and figure out where this thought came from. Walk your child through the feelings held and unpick them. Make it real and human.
- When your child explores a style of dress or music from a different ethnicity, bring this up and talk about it. Learning about cultural

appropriation and appreciation is essential as your child separates from you and enters the world (see page 202).

It is vital to incorporate race and racism into our talks with children. It creates a genuine interest in the world around us and the human race. These conversations should happen consistently and form a regular part of their everyday life, for example making a poster in November for the window that says 'Happy Diwali' to passers-by or including an unknown food in your food shop and trying it together to see if you like it – who can guess where it originates from? Try exploring your child's interests (such as their beloved football team) from the point of race – how many players have a heritage that's different to theirs? Show an interest in their latest music tastes and wonder out loud where that style of music comes from. If you sit and share a meal, encourage the kids to choose a person, country or religion to discuss.

Race doesn't have to be complicated. But it does have to be present. We, as parents, have the power to do that. It's our duty if the world is going to change.

Lucy Dixon is a parent specialist supporting parents, whilst providing evidence-based processes, to make family life easier. She works in partnership to undo unhelpful patterns and ensuring they can be the best parents they can be.

Scenario – based on a lived experience of my mum

A child is walking in the supermarket with her parent. She spots a person with brown skin. She runs up to the person and says, 'Are you made of chocolate? You are the same colour as my chocolate bar.'

- How would you respond?
- How would you feel?
- What would you say or do?
- How would you address the person they were referring to?

Children are naturally curious, unapologetically honest and simply say it as they see it. For many White people, the natural instinct is to say shush or pull our child away for fear of embarrassment. But this would be a missed opportunity for exploration and discussion about race and skin tones and the beautiful hues of colour that exist in our world. Shutting down the conversation may send signals that talking about race is not OK and that it is a taboo subject. This could lead to the conclusion that race is a bad thing. It's easy to see how this could happen, as the idea of race is usually associated with Black, Brown and racially minoritised people and not used to describe White folk.

It is important to take time to discuss what it means to point out a person's perceived colour and race, recognise that we may not be aware of a person's identity and are therefore making assumptions, and recognise that some people may be upset or offended when their race is pointed out.

Lived experience: Katie Friedman, leadership coach and neurodiversity trainer

As I was 'rescuing' the school in special measures (Saad, 2020), I pretty much renounced the education of my three sons, expecting the predominantly White school round the corner from my house to educate them for me. I knew that they would learn maths and English well at this school but that I would have to educate them about the wider world as the school's idea of education was narrow.

I am not sure when I thought this wider education would happen. When I finally realised how deliberate I would need to be about anti-racism, I was alarmed about the beliefs and assumptions that my ten-year-old had already formed about the few Black and Brown children in his class, likely systematically othered by teachers and students who didn't know how to talk about race or their White Privilege, privilege being not having to experience the daily othering because of the way their skin tone has been racialised.

I have lots of conversations with my children about privilege now. I have invested in lots of literature in order to teach them about White Privilege and appreciate bias in wider historical narratives.

My eldest was reading the paper and watching the news and noticed that predominantly White climate change demonstrations were referred to as 'protests' but Black Lives Matter demonstrations were 'riots'. The other morning he asked me why there were so few celebrated geniuses in history who were Black women. He went on to ask whether it was because there weren't any or that they weren't 'noticed'. We are slowly getting somewhere. It's never too late to wake up and start the practice of anti-racism.

Katie Friedman is the director of Gold Mind Neurodiversity Training Ltd, which provides neurodiversity training for leaders, educators and coaches. She is also a school leadership coach and a specialist trained ADHD coach.

Cultural appropriation versus cultural appreciation

As Lucy mentions on pages 199–200, a brilliant way for parents to speak with children about race is to explore different cultures, whether that's through discussing music, religious celebrations, clothes or food. This is true in the classroom as well. However, when doing this work, it is important to recognise the difference between cultural appreciation and cultural appropriation and to ensure children are also aware of this as they grow older.

To understand the difference between cultural appreciation and cultural appropriation, we must first understand the dynamic of power. Appropriation usually occurs when a dominant group takes from a marginalised or minoritised group. In addition, appropriation comes when something is 'borrowed' without any due care, respect or attention. The dominant group fails to take the time to research, develop their knowledge and understand the context of certain practices and why they are done in the way that they are. If there is an element of appreciation, it means the work takes on a different slant, because due care and attention has been paid and you've taken time to understand and respect the history, experiences and traditions of the culture you are exploring.

So, when discussing aspects of other cultures with children, don't introduce them as 'dressing-up games' or 'toys'. Together with the children, explore the relevant context and background of the traditions you are discussing, show how any items are used in authentic, real-life situations, and ensure discussions and activities are undertaken with respect.

I am grateful to Liz Pemberton, founder of The Black Nursery Manager, for sharing her expertise on cultural appropriation to inform this section.

Managing racist behaviour in parents and families

As the behaviour lead, I was often called to reception to support parents and families with concerns. As I arrived at reception on one occasion, I was met by some very upset parents who refused to talk to me and were very angry because they believed their child had been assaulted by another child and was being bullied. I explained my role (Assistant Principal for School Culture and Behaviour) and that I would be able to help. The parents responded with anger to my offer of help by saying, 'You can't help us. You are a Black b****. You are the same as the child who hurt my daughter.' The family were Eastern European and racialised as

White whereas the child who allegedly hurt their daughter was racialised as Black. The family assumed that as I was Black, I could not be impartial. Experiencing racism from a community that is also marginalised and discriminated against was hurtful and upsetting. The harder part was that it was parked and ignored with the focus being on the upset and frustration that the parents were feeling.

Racism impacts on differently racialised people and groups in different ways, and it is important to highlight that the UK definition of racism does not distinguish between communities. However, the experiences of racism will manifest differently in different communities. An area of racism that is often not discussed specifically is anti-Black racism. Anti-Blackness is defined as behaviours, attitudes and practices of individuals and institutions that work to dehumanise Black people to maintain White supremacy. It is a specific kind of racial prejudice directed towards Black people. Kim McIntosh, Senior Policy Officer at the Runnymede Trust, says: 'Anti-black racism is the specific exclusion and prejudice against people visibly (or perceived to be) of African descent – what most of us would commonly call black people' (quoted in Morris, 2020).

As ethnic groups are often clubbed together, individual experiences can often be misunderstood, ignored and marginalised. We see this in the use of terms such as BAME and People of Colour. Whilst these terms are commonly accepted as useful descriptors among many people, when my experiences as a Black woman are referred to as that of a Woman of Colour, it may undermine a specific experience that I have had as a Black woman. We sometimes see this in recruitment data when a school may not want to share that they do not have a Black member of staff and instead they use BAME or BME, which would include any staff member who is not White British.

Anti-Blackness creates a racial hierarchy that places people racialised as White at the top and people racialised as Black at the bottom. Therefore, People of Colour who are not Black can be complicit and play a part in the system of racism experienced by Black people. Many communities have bought into the anti-Black stereotypes in an attempt to be closer to Whiteness and the perceived benefits of White supremacy and power. Anti-Blackness may also be internalised and manifest itself in racially minoritised communities in the form of colourism. As defined by Dr Sarah L. Webb, 'colourism is the social marginalization and systemic oppression of people with darker skin tones and the privileging of people with lighter skin tones.' This may happen within different racialised ethnic groups and cultures. This form of oppression is rooted in racism, colonialism and White supremacy.

When I reflect on this moment, I have so many questions, especially in regards to the children who witnessed it. I ask myself, 'What were their thoughts on the interaction they had just witnessed?'

- What impact did this incident have on the children's racial literacy?
- Did it create a racial hierarchy in their mind?
- The parents felt it was acceptable to refer to my skin colour. Why? Did the family believe it was OK to refer to my skin colour at that moment?
- If a White senior leader had dealt with the incident (and the child accused was also White), would they have been a 'White b****'.
- What were their core beliefs about Black people?

Words do cause hurt, pain and trauma and the weaponisation of words like Black, the N-word and slavery in previous examples demonstrate the importance and need for racial literacy and clear policies and procedures in educational settings. These are words that many children and parents know will cause pain. Yet they still choose to use them to emphasise their point. Think about the following questions:

- What is it that we need to do better as educators to ensure that, in our school communities, there is a zero-tolerance policy on using racial slurs?
- How are you ensuring that you understand how racism is experienced in different communities?
- How can we be empathetic to parents and carers and still hold them accountable for the pain, upset and disrespect that is caused when staff are subject to racist abuse?
- How can we develop empathy from parents and carers, so they understand the suffering their words and actions cause staff who experience such reactions?
- What would your actions be if this happened in your setting?
- How would you handle this situation if it happened in your school?
- Would you challenge and support or would you be a bystander?
- As a leader, do you have clear policies and procedures in place to support staff that are fully embedded and consistently applied? How do you know that and can be sure?
- What would you do? Or on reflection, what do you need to do?

Summary

Key learning points

- It's essential that you consider the needs of all parents and carers, not just those who are White British, when you are writing school policies. Think in particular about your Prevent policy. How do your Black and Brown parents feel about this and how could you address any concerns?
- Support parents and carers in developing their own racial literacy and suggest steps they can take to talk to their children about race and racism at home.
- Ensure your policy on addressing racist behaviours covers incidents involving parents and carers in order to protect students and staff.

Key question

Did your parents or caregivers talk to you about race and racism?

a) Yes, all the time. In a positive and inclusive manner.

b) Yes. However, it was always like a warning or something to fear.

c) Sometimes. Typically, if something had happened, such as an event in the news.

d) Never.

How did this affect your relationship with other People of Colour? How has this shaped you as an educator? If you are a parent or caregiver, how does this affect the information your own children have access to?

Further self-reflection questions

1. As parents and carers, we have a responsibility to join the conversation about race and racism. However, support is often needed. As an educational setting, what support are you providing to ensure your parents and carers are racially literate?
2. How are you ensuring that staff and children are safe from racist abuse and harm from other parents?

Discussion points for staff meetings

- The recent Black Lives Matter movement caused much debate and discussion amongst parents. Some parents argued it was political and that schools are not a place for partisan views. Some parents felt that 'all lives matter'. Some felt that it was an American issue and that the UK was not racist.

  The Black Lives Matter movement was making it clear that all lives matter, including the lives of Black people. Even though slavery was abolished some 400 years ago, Black people are still experiencing systemic and structural racism which is impacting their lives today. Black people are not asking for better treatment, just to be treated with equal value.

  How are you supporting these discussions with your children? Are you discussing other similar movements such as #StopAsianHate, which was primarily a response from people of East and South-East Asian descent to an increase in racist incidents during the Covid-19 pandemic?

Thank you to all of you who made it to the end. It has been a journey… It is now your turn. What steps will you take to ensure that you are an anti-racist educator?

References

Abdi, M., 'Our services', https://ma-consultancy.co.uk/services

Abdi, M. (2021), 'Language is important: Why we are moving away from the terms "allyship" and "privilege" in our work', https://ma-consultancy.co.uk/blog/language-is-important-why-we-will-no-longer-use-allyship-and-privilege-in-our-work

Aboud, F. E. (2008), 'A social-cognitive developmental theory of prejudice', in S. M. Quintana and C. McKown (Eds.), *Handbook of Race, Racism, and the Developing Child*. Hoboken, NJ: John Wiley & Sons, pp. 55–71.

Advance HE (2017), 'Equality in higher education: statistical report 2017', www.advance-he.ac.uk/knowledge-hub/equality-higher-education-statistical-report-2017

Advance HE, (2020a), 'Equality and higher education – Staff statistical report 2020', www.advance-he.ac.uk/knowledge-hub/equality-higher-education-statistical-report-2020

Advance HE, (2020b), 'Equality and higher education – Student statistical report 2020', www.advance-he.ac.uk/knowledge-hub/equality-higher-education-statistical-report-2020

Akala (2018), *Natives: Race and class in the ruins of empire*. London: Two Roads.

Almquist, E. M. (1975), 'Untangling the effects of race and sex: The disadvantaged status of Black women', *Social Science Quarterly*, 56, (1), 129–142.

Anderson, L., Gatwiri, K., Riley, L. and Townsend-Cross, M. (2020), '9 tips teachers can use when talking about racism', *The Conversation*, https://theconversation.com/9-tips-teachers-can-use-when-talking-about-racism-140837

Annamma, S. A., Jackson, D. D. and Morrison, D. (2017), 'Conceptualizing color-evasiveness: Using dis/ability critical race theory to expand a color-blind racial ideology in education and society', *Race Ethnicity and Education*, 20, (2), 147–162.

Anzures, G., Quinn, P. C., Pascalis, O., Slater, A. M. and Lee, K. (2013), 'Development of own-race biases', *Visual Cognition*, 21, (9–10), 1165–1182.

Asthana, A. and Mason, R. (2016), 'Nigel Farage accused of "age-old racist" claim in linking migrants to sexual assault', *Guardian*, www.theguardian.com/politics/2016/jun/06/nigel-farage-accused-of-age-old-racist-claim-in-linking-migrants-to-sexual-assault

Auliq-Ice, O. (2019), 'When you are accustomed to privilege, equality feels like oppression', Tumblr, https://auliqice.tumblr.com

Balibar, E. and Wallerstein, I. (1991), *Race, Nation and Class*. London: Verso.

Bernard, D. L., Smith, Q. and Lanier, P. (2021), 'Racial discrimination and other adverse childhood experiences as risk factors for internalizing mental health concerns among Black youth', *Journal of Traumatic Stress*.

BBC News (2018), 'Lack of black teachers in Bristol "shocking"', www.bbc.co.uk/news/av/uk-england-bristol-45394186

Berners-Lee, T. (2006), 'Isn't it semantic?', interview with Brian Runciman, *BCS*, www.bcs.org/articles-opinion-and-research/isnt-it-semantic

Bhopal, K. (2018), *White Privilege: The myth of a post-racial society*. Bristol: Policy Press.

Billante, J. and Hadad, C. (2010), 'Study: White and black children biased toward lighter skin', *CNN*, http://edition.cnn.com/2010/US/05/13/doll.study/index.html

Bramble, S. (2020), 'Why representation matters in your workplace and beyond – Lessons from Wakanda', *Mental Health at Work*, www.mentalhealthatwork.org.uk/blog/why-representation-matters-in-your-workplace-and-beyond-lessons-from-wakanda

Burke, B. (2004), 'bell hooks on education', *The Encyclopedia of Pedagogy and Informal Education*, https://infed.org/mobi/bell-hooks-on-education/

Butler, J. (1990), *Gender Trouble: Feminism and the subversion of identity*. New York, NY; London: Routledge.

Centre for Literacy in Primary Education (2021), 'Reflecting realities: Survey of ethnic representation within UK children's literature 2020', https://clpe.org.uk/system/files/2021-11/CLPE%20Reflecting%20Realities%20Report%202021.pdf

Chamine, S. (2012), *Positive Intelligence: Why only 20% of teams and individuals achieve their true potential and how you can achieve yours*. Austin, TX: Greenleaf Book Group.

Chetty, D., Coles, F., Johns-Shepherd, L., Lander, V., Parker, N., Bold, M. and Sands O'Connor, K. (2020), 'Reflecting realities: Survey of ethnic representation within UK children's literature 2019'. London: Centre for Literacy in Literacy Education.

Citizens Advice, 'Race discrimination', www.citizensadvice.org.uk/law-and-courts/discrimination/protected-characteristics/race-discrimination

Clark, K. B. and Clark, M. P. (1947), 'Racial identification and preference among negro children', in E. L. Hartley (Ed.), *Readings in Social Psychology*. New York, NY: Holt, Rinehart, and Winston.

Commission on Race and Ethnic Disparities (2021), 'Commission on Race and Ethnic Disparities: The report', https://www.gov.uk/government/publications/the-report-of-the-commission-on-race-and-ethnic-disparities

Commons Education Committee (2021), 'The forgotten: How White working-class pupils have been let down, and how to change it', https://publications.parliament.uk/pa/cm5802/cmselect/cmeduc/85/8502.htm

Conkbayir, M. (2017), *Early Childhood and Neuroscience: Theory, research and implications for practice*. London: Bloomsbury.

Crenshaw, K. (1989), 'Demarginalizing the intersection of race and sex: A Black feminist critique of antidiscrimination doctrine, feminist theory and antiracist politics', *University of Chicago Legal Forum*, 1989, (1), 139–167.

Crown Prosecution Service (2022), 'Racist and religious hate crime – prosecution guidance', www.cps.gov.uk/legal-guidance/racist-and-religious-hate-crime-prosecution-guidance

Decety, J. (2020), *The Social Brain*. London: MIT Press.

Department for Education (2014a), 'National curriculum in England: Framework for key stages 1 to 4', www.gov.uk/government/publications/national-curriculum-in-england-framework-for-key-stages-1-to-4/the-national-curriculum-in-england-framework-for-key-stages-1-to-4

Department for Education (2014b), 'The Equality Act 2010 and schools', www.gov.uk/government/publications/equality-act-2010-advice-for-schools

Department for Education (2014c), 'Guidance on promoting British values in schools published', www.gov.uk/government/news/guidance-on-promoting-british-values-in-schools-published

Department for Education (2019), 'Early years foundation stage profile results: 2018 to 2019', www.gov.uk/government/statistics/early-years-foundation-stage-profile-results-2018-to-2019

Department for Education (2020a), 'Permanent and fixed-period exclusions in England: 2018 to 2019', www.gov.uk/government/statistics/permanent-and-fixed-period-exclusions-in-england-2018-to-2019

Department for Education (2020b), 'Development matters: Non-statutory guidance for the Early Years Foundation Stage', www.gov.uk/government/publications/development-matters--2

Department for Education (2020c), 'Personal, social, health and economic (PSHE) education', www.gov.uk/government/publications/personal-social-health-and-economic-education-pshe/personal-social-health-and-economic-pshe-education

Department for Education (2021a), 'School workforce in England: Reporting year 2020', https://explore-education-statistics.service.gov.uk/find-statistics/school-workforce-in-england

Department for Education (2021b), 'Schools, pupils and their characteristics', https://explore-education-statistics.service.gov.uk/find-statistics/school-pupils-and-their-characteristics

Department for Education (2021c), 'Keeping children safe in education', www.gov.uk/government/publications/keeping-children-safe-in-education--2

Department for Education (2021d), 'Teachers' standards', www.gov.uk/government/publications/teachers-standards

Department for Education (2021e), 'Early career framework', www.gov.uk/government/collections/early-career-framework-reforms

Department for Education (2022), 'Political impartiality in schools', www.gov.uk/government/publications/political-impartiality-in-schools/political-impartiality-in-schools

Department for Education and Race Disparity Unit (2018), 'Statement of intent on the diversity of the teaching workforce – setting the case for a diverse teaching workforce', www.gov.uk/government/publications/diversity-of-the-teaching-workforce-statement-of-intent

Ditzler, J. S. (2006), *Your Best Year Yet! A proven method for making the next 12 months your most successful ever.* London: HarperElement.

Du Bois, W. (1903), *The Souls of Black Folk: Essays and sketches.* Chicago, IL: A. C. McClurg & Co.

Duffy, N. (2020), 'Gavin Williamson rejects calls to "decolonise" history curriculum, saying Britons should be "proud of our history"', *inews.co.uk*, https://inews.co.uk/news/education/gavin-williamson-british-history-decolonise-blm-reject-empire-451290

Early Education (2012), *Development matters in the Early Years Foundation Stage (EYFS).* London: Department for Education, www.foundationyears.org.uk/files/2012/03/Development-Matters-FINAL-PRINT-AMENDED.pdf

Evelyn, K. (2020), '"Like I wasn't there": climate activist Vanessa Nakate on being erased from a movement', *Guardian*, www.theguardian.com/world/2020/jan/29/vanessa-nakate-interview-climate-activism-cropped-photo-davos

Fanon, F. (1952), *Peau noir, masques blancs.* Paris: Editions du Seuil.

Frankenberg, R. (1993), *White Women, Race Matters.* Minneapolis, MN: University of Minnesota Press.

Froehle, C. M. (2016), 'The evolution of an accidental meme', *Medium*, https://medium.com/@CRA1G/the-evolution-of-an-accidental-meme-ddc4e139e0e4

Funk, C. and Parker, K. (2018), 'Blacks in STEM jobs are especially concerned about diversity and discrimination in the workplace', *Women and Men in STEM Often at Odds over Workplace Equity*, www.pewresearch.org/social-trends/2018/01/09/blacks-in-stem-jobs-are-especially-concerned-about-diversity-and-discrimination-in-the-workplace

Gillborn, D. (2008), *Racism and Education.* London: Routledge.

Gilroy, P. (1987), *There Ain't No Black in the Union Jack: The cultural politics of race and nation.* London: Hutchinson.

Gilroy, P. (1993), *The Black Atlantic.* London: Verso.

Grosfoguel, R. (2013), 'The structure of knowledge in westernised universities: Epistemic racism/sexism and the four genocides/epistemicides', *Human Architecture: Journal of the Sociology of Self-Knowledge*, 1, (1), 73–90.

Harding, E. (2021), 'Schools must not teach children that white privilege is a fact, Education Secretary Nadhim Zahawi warns', *Daily Mail*, www.dailymail.co.uk/news/article-10118333/amp/Schools-not-teach-children-white-privilege-fact-Education-Secretary-warns.html

Henry-Allain, L. (2021), *My Skin, Your Skin*. London: Ladybird.

Her Majesty's Inspectorate (1989), 'Curriculum Matters 14: Personal and social education from 5 to 16', www.educationengland.org.uk/documents/hmi-curricmatters/pse.html

Hirschfeld, L. A. (2008), 'Children's developing conceptions of race', in S. M. Quintana and C. McKown (Eds.), *Handbook of Race, Racism, and the Developing Child*. Hoboken, NJ: John Wiley & Sons, pp. 37–54.

hooks, b. (1994), *Teaching to Transgress: Education as the practice of freedom*. Abingdon: Routledge.

Imani, B. (2021), *Read This to Get Smarter*. New York, NY: Ten Speed Press.

Kelly, D. J., Quinn, P. C., Slater, A. M., Lee, K., Gibson, A., Smith, M., Ge, L. and Pascalis, O. (2005), 'Three-month-olds, but not newborns, prefer own-race faces', *Developmental Science*, 8, (6), F31–6.

Kendi, I. (2019), *How to Be an Antiracist*. London: Penguin Random House.

Kimmel, T. (2005), *Grace-Based Parenting: Set your family tree*. Nashville, TN: Thomas Nelson.

Knight, M., Bunch, K., Tuffnell, D., Shakespeare, J. Kotnis, R., Kenyon, S. and Kurinczuk, J. J. (2020), 'Saving lives, improving mothers' care', MBRRACE-UK, www.npeu.ox.ac.uk/assets/downloads/mbrrace-uk/reports/maternal-report-2020/MBRRACE-UK_Maternal_Report_Dec_2020_v10_ONLINE_VERSION_1404.pdf

Knowles, C. (2003), *Race and Social Analysis*. London: Sage Publications.

Ladson-Billings, G. (2018), 'The importance of "White students having Black teachers"', *Education Week*, www.edweek.org/education/opinion-the-importance-of-white-students-having-black-teachers-gloria-ladson-billings-on-education/2018/02

LDF, 'A revealing experiment: Brown v. Board and "The Doll Test"', www.naacpldf.org/ldf-celebrates-60th-anniversary-brown-v-board-education/significance-doll-test

Leading Routes (2019), 'The broken pipeline – barriers to Black PhD students accessing research council funding', https://leadingroutes.org/mdocs-posts/the-broken-pipeline-barriers-to-black-students-accessing-research-council-funding

Leonardo, Z. (2009), *Race, Whiteness, and Education*. New York, NY; London: Routledge.

Lorde, A. (2017), *Your Silence Will Not Protect You*. London: Silver Press.

Lorde, A. (2018), *The Master's Tools Will Never Dismantle the Master's House*. London: Penguin.

Lothian-McLean, M. (2020), 'Fury as Afua Hirsch calls out Britain's racism and Nick Ferrari asks: "Why do you stay in this country?"', *Indy100*, www.indy100.com/news/afua-hirsch-nick-ferrari-sky-news-statues-racism-black-lives-matter-9558071

Luthar, S., Burack, J., Cicchetti, D. and Weisz, J. (1997), *Developmental Psychology: Perspectives on adjustment, risk and disorder*. Cambridge: Cambridge University Press.

MacNevin, M. and Berman, R. (2016), 'The Black baby doll doesn't fit the disconnect between early childhood diversity policy, early childhood educator practice, and children's play', *Early Child Development and Care*, 187, (5–6), 827–839.

Mandela, N. (1990), Speech at Madison Park High School. 23 June. Boston, MA.

Mandela, N. (1994), *Long Walk to Freedom*. London: Little, Brown and Company.

Mann, A., Denis, V., Schleicher, A., Ekhtiari, H., Forsyth, T., Liu, E. and Chambers, N. (2020), 'Dream jobs? Teenagers' career aspirations and the future of work', *OECD*, www.oecd.org/berlin/publikationen/Dream-Jobs.pdf

May, S. (1999), *Critical Multiculturalism: Rethinking multicultural and antiracist education*. Abingdon: Routledge.

McIntosh, P. (1989), 'White Privilege: Unpacking the invisible knapsack', *Peace and Freedom Magazine*, July/August, pp. 10–12.

McIntyre, N., Parveen, N. and Thomas, T. (2021), 'Exclusion rates five times higher for black Caribbean pupils in parts of England', www.theguardian.com/education/2021/mar/24/exclusion-rates-black-caribbean-pupils-england

Menakem, R. (2021), *My Grandmother's Hands*. London: Penguin.

Merrick, R. (2021), 'Schools minister rejects lessons about colonialism and slave trade in case they "lower standards"', *Independent*, www.independent.co.uk/news/uk/politics/school-compulsory-lessons-colony-slave-trade-b1807571.html

Mlynek, A. (2017), 'How to talk to kids about racism: An age-by-age guide', www.todaysparent.com/family/parenting/how-to-talk-to-kids-about-racism-an-age-by-age-guide

Morris, N. (2020), '"Anti-blackness" is a form of racism that is specifically damaging for black people', *Metro*, https://metro.co.uk/2020/03/20/what-is-anti-blackness-12279678

Morrow, W. (2009), *Bounds of Democracy: Epistemological access in higher education*. Cape Town: HSRC Press.

Murray, J. (2020), 'Teaching white privilege as uncontested fact is illegal, minister says', *Guardian*, www.theguardian.com/world/2020/oct/20/teaching-white-privilege-is-a-fact-breaks-the-law-minister-says

Myhre, K. T. (2018), *A Love Song, A Death Rattle, A Battle Cry*. Minneapolis, MN: Button Poetry.

Naughton, G. M. and Davis, K. (eds.) (2009), *Race and Early Childhood Education: An international approach to identity, politics, and pedagogy*. Basingstoke: Palgrave Macmillan.

Ofsted (2011), 'Hamstead Hall Community Learning Centre: Inspection report', https://files.ofsted.gov.uk/v1/file/1965801

Oxford Dictionaries, 'role model', www.lexico.com/definition/role_model

Oxford Dictionaries, 'decolonise', www.lexico.com/definition/decolonise

Pease, B. (2010), *Undoing Privilege: Unearned advantage in a divided world*. London: Zed Books.

Pelt-Willis, T. (2021), 'The moment we realized: Triple consciousness and the intersectionality of race, gender and sexuality in 20th and 21st century African American women', https://hdl.handle.net/11244/331408

Perszyk, D. R., Lei, R. F., Bodenhausen, G. V., Richeson, J. A. and Waxman, S. R. (2019), 'Bias at the intersection of race and gender: Evidence from preschool-aged children', *Developmental Science*, 22, (3), e12788.

Pierson, R. (2013), 'Every kid needs a champion', *TED Talk*, www.ted.com/talks/rita_pierson_every_kid_needs_a_champion

PSHE Association, 'Why PSHE matters', www.pshe-association.org.uk/what-we-do/why-pshe-matters

PSHE Association (2020), 'Programme of study for PSHE education: Key Stages 1–5', https://pshe-association.org.uk/curriculum-and-resources/resources/programme-study-pshe-education-key-stages-1%E2%80%935

Race Reflections, https://racereflections.co.uk

Rippon, G. (2019), *The Gendered Brain: The new neuroscience that shatters the myth of the female brain*. London: Random House.

Rollock, N. (2018), 'Black female professors', https://nicolarollock.com/white-allies

Ruiz, D. M. (2018), *The Four Agreements: A Toltec Wisdom Book*. San Rafael, CA: Amber-Allen.

Rumbold, A. (1990), 'The Rumbold report: Starting with quality', www.educationengland.org.uk/documents/rumbold/rumbold1990.html

Runnymede Trust (2017), 'Bristol: a city divided?', www.runnymedetrust.org/uploads/CoDE%20Briefing%20Bristol%20v2.pdf

Saad, L. (2020), *Me and White Supremacy: How to recognise your privilege, combat racism and change the world*. London: Hachette.

Shackle, S. (2017), 'Trojan horse: the real story behind the fake "Islamic plot" to take over schools', *Guardian*, www.theguardian.com/world/2017/sep/01/trojan-horse-the-real-story-behind-the-fake-islamic-plot-to-take-over-schools

Siraj-Blatchford, I. and Clarke, P. (2000), *Supporting Identity, Diversity and Language in the Early Years*. Buckingham: Open University Press.

Sky News (2020), 'George Floyd death: Health Secretary Matt Hancock quizzed on cabinet diversity', https://news.sky.com/video/george-floyd-death-health-secretary-matt-hancock-quizzed-on-cabinet-diversity-12002134

SOAS (2018), 'Decolonising SOAS: Learning and teaching toolkit for programme and module convenors', https://blogs.soas.ac.uk/decolonisingsoas/files/2018/10/Decolonising-SOAS-Learning-and-Teaching-Toolkit-AB.pdf

Spencer, O. (2014), 'Octavia Spencer on Hollywood and race: The film roles I'm offered are too small'. Interview with Marlow Stern, *The Daily Beast*, www.thedailybeast.com/octavia-spencer-on-hollywood-and-race-the-film-roles-im-offered-are-too-small

Sue, D. W., 'Microaggression: More than just race', www.uua.org/files/pdf/m/microaggressions_by_derald_wing_sue_ph.d._.pdf

The African Doctor (2016). [Film]. Julien Rambaldi (dir.). France: Mars Films.

Thomas, A. (2019), 'Why representation really matters', *TEDx Bristol*, www.ted.com/talks/aisha_thomas_why_representation_really_matters

Thunberg, G. (2019), Speech at the United Nations Climate Action Summit, 23 September. UN Headquarters, New York, NY, www.un.org/development/desa/youth/news/2019/09/greta-thunberg

Uberoi, E. and Lees, R. (2020), 'Ethnic diversity in politics and public life', House of Commons Library, https://researchbriefings.files.parliament.uk/documents/SN01156/SN01156.pdf

UCL Institute of Education (2020), '46% of all schools in England have no BAME teachers', www.ucl.ac.uk/ioe/news/2020/dec/46-all-schools-england-have-no-bame-teachers

UNICEF, 'The United Nations Convention on the Rights of the Child', www.unicef.org.uk/what-we-do/un-convention-child-rights

United Nations (1989), 'Convention on the Rights of the Child', www.ohchr.org/en/professionalinterest/pages/crc.aspx

Universities UK, 'Black, Asian and Minority Ethnic student attainment at UK universities: #ClosingtheGap', www.universitiesuk.ac.uk/sites/default/files/field/downloads/2021-07/bame-student-attainment.pdf

Wallace, D. and Joseph-Salisbury, R. (2021), 'How, still, is the Black Caribbean child made educationally subnormal in the English school system?', *Ethnic and Racial Studies*.

Weale, S. (2020), 'Ofsted chief resists calls to make England school curriculum more diverse', *Guardian*, www.theguardian.com/education/2020/dec/01/england-ofsted-chief-resists-calls-to-make-curriculum-more-diverse

Webb, S. L., 'Colorism Healing', https://colorismhealing.com

Williams, Z. (2015), 'Katie Hopkins calling migrants vermin recalls the darkest events of history', *Guardian*, www.theguardian.com/commentisfree/2015/apr/19/katie-hopkins-migrants-vermin-darkest-history-drownings

Williams, A. (2016), 'Why we should talk to children about race', *The Conversation*, https://theconversation.com/why-we-should-talk-to-children-about-race-59615

Winkler, E. N. (2009), 'Children are not colorblind: How young children learn race', *PACE*, 3, (3).

World Economic Forum (2019), 'HR4.0: Shaping people strategies in the fourth industrial revolution', www3.weforum.org/docs/WEF_NES_Whitepaper_HR4.0.pdf

Young Citizens, 'British values', www.youngcitizens.org/resources/citizenship/british-values

Index